MW01644352

SPIRIT VIGILANTE

Telling My Truth to Help You Live Yours

LINDSEY
VAN WAGNER

Published in the United States by Haven 101 Press

Photography: Brandon Chang
Cover layout and design: H9D Studio

 The author of this book does not provide medical advice or prescribe the use of any technique as a form of treatment for physical, emotional, or medical problems, without the advice of a physician. Always seek the advice of a qualified healthcare provider with questions regarding a medical condition or treatment and before undertaking a new health regimen.

ISBN: 979-8-9915989-1-0 pbk
ISBN: 979-8-9915989-4-1 hbk
ISBN: 979-8-9915989-2-7 ebk

Haven 101 Press

For every version of yourself
who has kept you going
through this wild, beautiful,
terrifying, incredible life...

I see you.

CONTENTS

Foreword

by
Trina C. Ulrich, MD, CHC, CISSN

More than seven years ago, as a passionate physician and professor educating and empowering others to continually improve health, I found myself dealing with a unique graduate student in one of my courses. Changes in Health Behavior was the title of the course, and author, Lindsey Van Wagner, was the student pursuing a master's degree in nutrition education at American University. Why was Lindsey unique? There's so much to share!

My first impression of Lindsey was her sense of adventure. Her fun-loving dedication to juggling life while experiencing catastrophic hurricanes in St. Croix and continuing to complete assignments for our graduate-level course, drew me in to connect and support her situation. Obviously, I also noticed her stellar academic performance and deep understanding of the material at hand, which I admit tends to also draw in a professor. I'll always remember the day Lindsey emailed me sharing that her course assignments would be turned in as soon she found a way to reach the one café on the entire island with power. I shared my cell phone number in hopes our communication would be easier. The rest is history.

After graduation, Lindsey's innate fervor to combine the fields of nutrition education and psychology was palpable. As she dove into her next academic adventure, the challenges, hiccups, and enormous roadblocks Lindsey encountered along her journey are a testament to how one perseveres and discovers their true self. Fast forward to the present, Lindsey's dedication to her growth and helping others has translated to great success in her entrepreneurial endeavors, which include authoring books, creating writing workshops, leading retreats, teaching the same course I taught her at American University, and opening a business for fellow health and wellness professionals to hold a physical space to support clients.

I feel honored to teach graduate students, like Lindsey, who are gifted with a certain energy to connect and support others. Years ago, while working as a clinical physician, my need to discover why some patients created the change necessary to improve their health, while others did not, led me to further my studies in Integrative Nutrition. These studies combined a deep dive into the interplay between nutrition science, human physiology, behavior change, and health psychology. I learned that prescribing change or telling others what to do tends to create short-lived improvement. Educating and igniting another's intrinsic motivation leads to more successful and lasting change and implementation. Furthermore, long-term improvements in health behavior toward oneself lead to a domino effect and further improvements in various aspects of life. Perhaps we should call it a ripple effect. And Lindsey spreads her ripple effect far and wide.

It is obvious Lindsey realizes change may feel elusive to some and this is why she wrote *Spirit Vigilante*, a heartfelt journey that has a transformative power. Be prepared to discover how Lindsey's ripple effect may become instilled into your own life journey. This book offers more than just a story; it is a compassionate and supportive guide through the complexities of human behavior. Empowering others to create change in their own lives is an art and Lindsey's talent to do this is real.

At its core, *Spirit Vigilante* brings to light the psychology behind behavior change—what drives us, what holds us back, and how we can ultimately rise above and rediscover our true selves. The book invites readers to look deeper into their motivations, fears, and desires. In these pages, the connection between the courage to choose and the knowledge to understand how change unfolds, is continuous and can bring contentment to the soul, so we all may discover and extend our own unique ripple effects.

Spirit Vigilante
/ˈspirət vijəˈlan(t)ē/ noun

spirit = a force within a human being thought to give the body life, energy, and power.

vigilante = the word itself is borrowed from the Spanish word of the same spelling that means "watchman" or "guard," traced back to the word *vigilare* which means "to keep awake."

As Spirit Vigilantes, we guard our souls. We are alert and aware. We are dedicated to protecting ourselves as we expand our energy, even if society at large may not understand or agree with our actions. Spiritual wellness is an individual and personal endeavor. Vigilantes often work quietly behind the scenes, but make no mistake, we are putting in the sweat and tears. Join our movement as you embark on a transformational journey to uncover your hidden gifts, reclaim your power, and change your world. You are the architect of your own healing, and we are here to support you every step of the way, cheering you on as you begin to recognize and implement your soul's brilliance. You have the power to transform into your full potential and become the main character of your life. Trust your Truth. Claim justice for your soul.

Let's Begin

In 2016, a few days after Christmas, I had to ask myself how I landed in 7 West, the psychiatric unit of Sibley Memorial Hospital in Washington, DC. I had the car, the cushy federal government job, all the appropriate material trappings. The boxes were neatly checked. But I was living a double life. Riddled with anxiety and emptiness, I had been wandering aimlessly into a gray foggy abyss that was swallowing me whole. I wanted it all to end.

Struggling to balance bipolar disorder with my newfound sobriety, consciousness seemed intolerable. The mental and emotional angst I had been suppressing with drugs and alcohol were quickly rising to the surface. I felt like a bomb waiting to explode. I figured I had finally reached the end of my life, that it was my natural time to go. In the twenty-nine years I had been on this earth, I had seen what I needed to see. Little did I know, life was just getting started. What I saw then as a break*down* was actually a break*through* that saved my life and opened the door for the next phase of my journey.

This source of anxiety—lack of direction and a longing for clarity and meaning—insidiously manifests in a myriad of ways. Complacency in our careers, low self-worth, and addictive behaviors that numb our feelings of depression and confusion. Blinded by fear and uncertainty, we refuse to go against the grain of convention and status quo, and we do not listen to our inner voice which knows the truth.

My Vision for You

You are so much farther along in your journey than you think. You wouldn't have gravitated toward this book otherwise. There is a reason it found you at this exact moment in time. You are ready to hear these words. What does "ready" mean? Your brain may not feel ready, but your soul is. So, don't wait. Mood follows action.

I want you to feel free. . . free to be you. I want you to take life less seriously and let it be a little bit easier and a lot more fun. This freedom, this allowance to live in accordance with your true nature is a natural high that no drug, drink, dessert, pleasure, person, or addiction can come close to matching. This experience comes from within, and it never runs out.

You aren't turning into someone new; you're returning to who you already are and always have been since the beginning of time and creation. Just as much as you want to uncover your destiny, it is waiting to be uncovered. This is your roadmap. As the journey unfolds it will meet you and carry you. It has a life of its own that is influenced by far more than your brain and body.

Spirit Vigilantism is a movement devoted to Truth. When I look back at all the pivotal incidents, reroutes, and transitions in my life, Truth is the common denominator—escaping truth, denying truth, covering the truth, running from the truth, and then eventually returning to truth, reuniting with truth, and integrating truth into my life again. My truth.

Now you are invited to embark on this journey.

Why trust *me*? I am an expert in health psychology, and I educate individuals and groups in areas such as nutrition and lifestyle modifications, yogic philosophy, general wellness, and spiritual principles of healing. I am an adjunct professor at American

University for the Department of Health Studies with a specialization in behavior change. I also operate a wellness studio for holistic healing in Rockville, Maryland. More importantly, I have lived this journey. I can sit with you in the trenches of battle because I know your pain. The only way for me to make sense of what I have overcome is to share it with you. There are many resources out there, so I sincerely thank you for choosing this one.

There is one major requirement I urge of you: be gentle with yourself. This is non-negotiable. Listen to yourself. No one knows you better than you do. Let yourself have feelings and worries and emotions and never apologize for them.

If you start crying in public and it makes other people uncomfortable, do not say sorry. Do not ask forgiveness for having a human moment. When you show up unapologetically yourself, unapologetically human—on the good days and the bad—you inspire others.

You are the only person in the world who has been there for yourself every day, on the beautiful mornings all the way through the sleepless nights. You have shown up. You have fought the battles. And you deserve to be here.

You can read these words as slowly or as quickly as you need. The lessons and phases will always be relevant no matter where you are on your journey. Everyone moves at different paces when enacting sustainable and realistic change and transformation.

Spirit Vigilante is a vehicle that will take you through these eight phases and guide you toward your highest potential. I offer the methods that have proved tried and true for me. My mission is to help those struggling by sharing what happened, what I did about it, and what my life is like now. Each chapter presents a reflection on the relevant and overarching components of that phase of growth and offers practices for real-life application using models and exercises designed specifically for this book. Brief conclusions wrap up the chapter with a key takeaway, linking concepts in the subsequent phases. Throughout, you will encounter this symbol 🔍, indicating a particular concept or methodology that can be investigated more deeply in the Explore section found at the end of the book. These pages are intended to allow you to return to topics that pique your interest and dive deeper into analysis at your leisure without losing sight of the overall narrative.

The stories I share in the chapters to come capture emotional pain, mental illness, addiction, darkness, loss of self, suicidal ideation, criminal prosecution, identity crises, and ultimately an awakening to peace and personal triumph. My story[1] is here to provide context for the real-life examples of problems and solutions we all face. While I hope my journey delivers an entertaining and engaging narrative (some moments will be heart-wrenching and others humorous), the personal aspects only serve as an outline to bring the philosophical abstractions to life. *You* get to color in your own hues, shades, stories, and patterns. I want you to walk away with a confident plan of action, one that makes you hopeful, encourages you to persevere, and reminds you again and again that you can overcome.

My words are meant to motivate, inspire, and empower you by raising your consciousness, self-awareness, and most importantly show you what you already know to be true (even if you don't know that you know).

---

[1] Some names have been changed to protect the privacy of the people involved.

8 Phases

Looking back on my life's trials and tribulations, I developed a Spirit-centered framework and methodology of lessons to support and strengthen the mind-body connection, melding the clinical and mystical, the logical and intuitive. These juxtapositions complement and corroborate one another, working in tandem rather than as opposing forces. The pillars of this framework were built from personal experience, social behavior research on health psychology, and motivation to change. Deep down we usually know the "right" thing to do to get to where or who we want to be, or at least a closer version, but it takes more than cut-and-dried knowledge to make a change. There has to be a personal and emotional connection to something deeper than logic and reason. *Sprit Vigilante* is your key to unlocking that door.

This book is divided into eight chapters, each dedicated to a different phase of growth. The number 8 is intentional, representing infinity ∞ and the cyclical nature of life's journey rather than a linear series of tasks with distinct start and end points.

"Notice" raises awareness around your unhealthy behaviors.

"Allow" guides you toward a willingness to open up so that the truth may enter.

"Shed" offers tips to chip away at the deep, stubborn layers of delusion.

"Uncover" helps you realize your true nature.

"Stabilize" assists in implementing personalized coping tools and healthy habits.

"Leap" opens your heart to let intuition guide your direction.

"Evolve" affirms your ability to access the natural flow of life and realign with your highest self.

"Ascend" is the moment you use your truth to share your message and gifts with the world.

The life events I share with you are not chronologically portrayed in a neat order. The steps aren't necessarily progressive from one to the next, nor are any dependent on another. Rather, they flow cyclically. The *Spirit Vigilante* framework is purposefully and strategically fluid, there is a method to my madness. This structure is reflective of life; we go through these phases in different situations, and there are various points of entry for the wisdom to flow through.

You can revisit these lessons over and over throughout different stages of your life, as you encounter obstacles and arrive at turning points. Once you trust this process and trust yourself, you will thrive on the consistency of this solution and the tools you can rely on. The way you use the tools may change over time, but the principles and precepts will remain effective. They aren't quick fixes or Band-Aids to make you feel better only for the moment. They are lifelong ongoing practices, but don't let that feel daunting. This is something to be excited about. Be here now and soak it all in.

A Personal Note

We all experience pain differently because we all experience life differently. My social identity is such that I am a white, American, abled, cisgender, college-educated female raised in an upper-middle-class family. I am privileged. The reason I can put these letters together to form words and sentences and paragraphs is because I was blessed with the resources to obtain an education. This is the only identity I have ever known and the only one I can report. I do not pretend to know hardship in ways that others do, but I strive to maintain a beginner's mind of cultural humility. I do my best every day to acknowledge social inequity and not perpetuate it.

My pain was not caused by poverty, racism, or stereotypes. My soul went dark, and I am grateful for the opportunities I had to get well—access to healthcare, a supportive family, and many other resources along the way. However, those things couldn't help me do the internal work. I had to make a true effort, and after putting a bunch of little steps together, I now wake up sober and alive in a completely different way. I enjoy deep friendships. I participate fully at family functions, and I have broken the mold to follow my dreams. I am someone who genuinely wants to help other people.

I can look the world square in the eye. I let myself take up space. I know my worth. I can go places by myself and dance even if no one else is. How is this possible when I am also the woman who couldn't get out of bed for days and once contemplated running in front of a bus? Most of life is a mystery. There is a lot more that we don't know than we do, so I will share my story and explain what I do understand, as well as what is anecdotally and clinically proven to help transform your life.

Spirit Steps

Throughout this book there will be sections labeled "Spirit Steps," marked with a star and sun symbol at both the opening and closing of the activity. This is your turn to reflect and put theory into action by applying the principles within these phases to your real life. I recommend using a special notebook and your favorite pen as we take this journey together. We are aiming for an interactive experience. A collaboration. A brand-new chapter for you, one to honor and treat with respect. More than just reading pretty words and feeling inspired, I want you to feel that you are taking practical action and attaining success. You can trust yourself to follow through. If you arrive at one of these sections, and you are reading the book on a train or somewhere you cannot immerse yourself into the experience, no problem. Mark the page and come back to it later.

Guiding Principles:

Embrace curiosity instead of cynicism.
Look at it as an experiment, you are the sample.
Turn your worry into wonder.
Claim hope instead of doubt.
Be present, life is about paying attention.
Be gentle with yourself. Listen to yourself.
No one else knows you better than you do.
Let yourself have feelings and worries and emotions and never apologize for them.
Keep an open mind, a humble heart, and a receiving Soul.

You are so much more powerful than the level at which you are operating. I am excited for you to discover this for yourself. My biggest hope is that you may live in your truth and your light and feel at peace every time you close your eyes at night.

You are instrumental to this book's existence. All the steps it took to get here—forcing myself to get up at two in the morning to meet deadlines, the diligent editing, the ideas rushing too fast for my fingers to keep up—were undertaken because I told myself I would do whatever it takes to help you. I wasn't going through these challenges solely for my own benefit and self-actualization, this was something way bigger. That is how powerful and important and significant *you* are.

I knew this book needed to land in your hands, that my words needed to find your eyes or your ears. It was not about me or my comfort or assuaging my fears or soothing my ego.

How did I get here?

Little steps. One day at a time. Faith. Trust. Hope. Love.

Let's take this walk together now, shall we?

Chapter One
Notice

/ˈnō-dəs/ verb
to observe or pay attention to something
I *notice* that the trees are beginning to blossom.

I sat in the waiting room of the stale, drab, fluorescent-lit psychiatrist's office, anxiously pecking at my phone. At the ripe old age of twenty-five, it wasn't my first time in the mental health treatment landscape and it wouldn't be my last.

I had been seeing Dr. G for several months now and our sessions were short. He asked about my symptoms, my mood, any side effects with the meds—the usual interrogation. In truth, I wasn't regularly taking the medication he prescribed, and due to my fragile mental state overlapping with the drinking overlapping with the marijuana overlapping with my chaotic behavior, I lacked any awareness of the effect they were having. At least, I felt better knowing I was doing something about my "issues." More importantly, as this appointment was precipitated by a bad drinking episode, it got my boyfriend off my back.

The Sunday prior I had arrived at Savannah's, a local dive bar in the suburbs of Maryland, just after eleven o'clock in the morning and ordered a bucket of long-neck Bud Lights. I was there to "watch the football game" and meet up with Jim—a man twice my age. We were both regulars. At this point, that was my idea of a friendship. I accepted all shots offered to me, especially Fireball whiskey. I loved how the combination of sweet cinnamon and pungent alcohol burned my throat.

The day became blurry and by early afternoon some dude wanted me to leave the bar with him. My beer goggles could make anyone look like Bradley Cooper and my drunken brain would convince me they were *the one,* and they clearly thought I was too. Why else would they be so kind as to invite me into their home? I started to follow him outside. Jim did not approve and came after us. I later learned that he kicked the entrance door down in the process. He yelled and threw my keys across the parking lot, which had been in his pocket because he didn't want me to drive.

The next memory I have is of sitting in the passenger seat of an unfamiliar car. I looked to my left. The bartender, Carrie, was staring back at me with her sweet big blue eyes. "Where is the next turn?"

"Oh, just up this way," my words sounded sloppy in my mouth.

I remember little else about that ride except that it was still light outside, and she took the street that runs parallel to the train tracks.

I stumbled into my house and sat on the floor. I was wearing a light pink shirt with turquoise block lettering that read *90210* on top of a black-and-white picture of Luke Perry. The neck was cut out, so it fell off my shoulder as I laid on the ground, staring up at the ceiling. Ben, my boyfriend at the time, was in the living room playing FIFA. He just sat there, holding his controller, and watched me for a few minutes.

"Where were you?"

"I was at the bar with Jim."

"Who even is that?"

I sighed, annoyed. "He's friends with Sam. You know Jim." Sam was my crush who lived across the street. This was all very healthy.

Ben walked away and I stayed on the ground. A few minutes later he came back and said, "Lindsey, you're an alcoholic. It's getting really bad. You need help."

Dude, you're being a drama queen, I thought to myself.

I sat in the chair across from Dr. G with my hands folded. I hated these types of offices. No desk between you and the practitioner. All that separated us was hollow air, as if we were having a casual conversation at a cocktail party waiting for someone to grace us with the hors d'oeuvre tray.

He looked down at his clipboard, "And how much are you drinking?"

"Oh, only on the weekends still." I hoped that's what I told him last time. I was having a hard time keeping up with my lies.

He looked at me with a blank stare and sighed, "And how *much* are you drinking on the weekends?"

"Hmmm, if I had to come up with an average, Friday and Saturday night, about five drinks each, so… ten drinks a week."

It seemed like a reasonable number since he already knew I was a drinker—not so low to be recognized as a flat-out lie, not too high to cause alarm. It was probably less than a quarter of the volume of alcohol I was actually consuming on a regular basis.

I rolled my shoulders back and held my head up high, a false air of confidence. Dr. G stood up, his intimidating six-foot-six frame towering over me. His eyes drifted away, "I can't see you anymore." He turned away from me and walked to his desk on the other side of the room.

"What?" I must have misheard him.

Even with his back turned, his exasperation was clear, "You won't stop drinking. You can't drink on these medications. You're a liability. Every appointment, you come back here and tell me that you're still getting drunk."

“I don’t understand. I’m not even drinking that much.”

He turned around and I sat doe eyed.

“Yes. You are. What you are describing is called binge drinking.” I quickly realized he wasn’t going to budge.

I stood, the top of my head not even reaching his shoulders and looked up at his graying beard and eyeglasses with thick black frames. “You’re going to stop seeing me because I am *too fucked up*?! What kind of doctor does that? What is wrong with you?” It didn’t cross my mind that his level of appall at my obvious lie or actual alcohol consumption might be a problem.

Dr. G’s voice and inflection didn’t waver. He maintained his composure as he said, “I had a patient die last summer and you are too high of a risk. You have bipolar disorder so you shouldn’t be drinking at all, and you are on several medications that are unsafe to combine with alcohol. You’re a liability. Find another doctor.”

Escape Routes and Denial

I did not find another doctor. In fact, I did the exact opposite. Spoiler alert: I drank more, and my self-pity escalated. I would not seek help for some time. I spent a lot of time in despair and confusion, about a decade, a period I call my Lost Years.

Looking back, I didn’t know who I was, and that question was too scary to face. College was over and school had been my identity for fifteen years. I had no way of measuring myself in this new world of my early twenties. No more handwritten A+ on the top of each assignment, adjacent to a scrawled “Great job!” or “Excellent work!”

Thinking back to that girl storming out of the psychiatrist’s office breaks my heart. She simply could not accept that alcohol might be her problem because, at the time, it was her only solution.

I didn't want to think about my life, so I created an alternate reality that made my waking moments bearable. Humans do this in more ways than one. It is sometimes difficult to feel, and we want to escape, even if this is all happening at a subconscious level. It is a human tendency to want to alter our perception or experience, in hopes of changing the unpleasant thoughts, emotions, sensations.

I refer to these unhealthy patterns as "escape routes," and they are not limited to classic cases of addiction. They can manifest in habits, relationships, or any behavior that has more authority over your willpower than does your inner spirit. Some common maladaptive escape routes that we see every day are binge-eating, dieting, shopping, gambling, scrolling social media, video games, alcohol and drugs, codependency (unhealthy relationship dynamics), workaholism, television/streaming, excessive sleeping, gossiping, obsessing, and the list goes on. Succumbing to these diversions is not a moral flaw or failure. Though the behaviors may differ, the desire to change one's reality is the same. More important than the specific behavior is the *why* behind the need to distract ourselves in such self-destructive ways.

The Antidote to Denial

These escape routes serve a purpose for our ego, which is why they are so persistent and difficult to identify and change. The ego is the inner image of yourself in the context of your external world, the part of the human personality experienced as the "self" or "I." One characteristic of the human condition is feeling a need to constantly defend, protect, and justify the ego. It is a security measure to make us feel safe in this world. When we let the ego lead rather than our truth, which is comprised of heart and soul, life can become unmanageable.

There is a reason we develop certain ego-driven patterns and continue reinforcing them until they are no longer helpful, and the pain of maintaining that false structure becomes uncomfortable and counterproductive. We all reach the impetus to change at different points, after whatever is needed to wake us up, but we don't have to go *all* the way to the lowest point before intervening. It is not necessary to wait until things go from bad to worse to have a reason to change or commit to improving your life. Self-exploration is the antidote to denial. It prompts us to observe and recognize the actions and mindsets that are blocking the light of our truest selves.

My instinct and compulsion to engage in some type of automatic behavior is based on a distinct feeling inside of me: *Ahh, something is making me uncomfortable; I need to change this right away!*

But some behaviors are not so time-sensitive or impulsive. They can be subtle, such as an obsession with getting that next material thing, or hitting that next milestone, and then the next, and then the next. *Once I get that promotion... once I get the newest Tesla... once the kids go to college... then, I will finally be happy. Once, once, once. Someday, someday, someday, I'll do what I want. I'll feel how I want. I will have made it.*

With all due respect, *when* will this day come?

That last goal you reached; did you get the satisfaction you were seeking? How long did that good feeling last?

Happiness cannot be found in external rewards. We overdo certain behaviors because we keep reaching for an elusive calm that can only come from within. We need to get curious about our patterns and what blocks us from that inner peace and freedom.

Are You Willing to Take a Look?

You don't have to change anything right now, just consider if some part of your life feels out of control. It may be completely obvious, or hiding in a place you least expect it. Get curious about your behaviors. Maybe your mind is telling you something is wrong, or you are feeling unsettled. Start small.

Asking these questions can be scary, but raising awareness is the first step to enacting change. We can't grow or make adjustments if we don't know what exactly is misaligned.

Think about that hard thing you are going through right now.

What came to mind as you read that statement? Was it something abstract like "I'm not good enough," or something more specific? "My best friend isn't talking to me, and the world won't feel right until they do."

In what area(s) of your life do you feel lost? This could be socially, overwhelmed by your events and engagements, or your profession, or maybe even one of your relationships. You might be in denial, just as I was with my alcoholism.

Some signs that the quicksand of denial had me in its grip? Repeatedly driving drunk and in blackouts, even after criminal charges for a DUI at age 21; concealing alcohol in a coffee thermos so people wouldn't know I was drinking; crashing into a parking gate because it wouldn't open fast enough and I wanted to get to the next bar (mimosas and Grey Goose are not a great mix); smoking marijuana on my lunch breaks on the property of a federally-owned-and-operated building; cheating on my live-in boyfriend with my neighbor who lived across the street. Any one of those could have been a turning point for me, but they had no effect on the course of my drinking and did not make a dent in the chaos of my irresponsible actions.

Spirit Steps

Consider and Reflect

Take several rounds of deep breaths, inhale through your nose and exhale through your mouth.

Ask yourself, "What behavior(s) might be inhibiting my growth—big or small?"

Sit comfortably and set a timer for at least five minutes. Close your eyes and observe what comes up in your mind and body. Be gentle.

Free-write without overthinking until you identify one behavior that might be an issue. Circle it.

Observe yourself for one week without trying to change anything, and record the frequency of that behavior while also taking note of the emotions around it—before, during, and/or after—and any other notes you think may be helpful to your self-discovery process. Check in with yourself a few times a day. For example, let's say the habit is smoking cigarettes. In the 6am-12pm row, you might check *Sometimes* because you tend to smoke in the morning with your coffee, but in the 12am-6am space, you would select *Rarely* because you are usually sleeping at that time. The *When* row all the way at the bottom is for you to fill in. It could be, *When [a particular person] is around* or *When I feel bored*, or *When* ______, you fill in the blank.

	Never	Rarely	Sometimes	Always
6am-12pm				
12pm-6pm				
6pm-12am				
12am-6am				
When ________				

In the second table below (and continued on the next page), record your emotional response to the behavior. How does it feel when you smoke that cigarette? The feelings shown in the table are just examples; come up with your own words and descriptions that feel like a better fit. Pay attention and allow whatever comes up. See if you notice any patterns or correlations. What are the associated emotions around this behavior? (before, during, after)

	Never	Rarely	Sometimes	Always
I feel guilty and/or ashamed				
I feel out of control				

Instant relief, but it is short-lived				
I feel ________				
I feel ________				
I feel ________				

Theory

Though we all have our own unique stories, there is value in looking through the lens of behavior research and universal conclusions drawn by the experts, especially if we are aiming to observe without judgment. These frameworks can serve as a launching point to act from a place of objectivity and neutral witnessing, as we apply effective practices to our own situations.

The Stages of Change

Do you want to change?

Why?

Is it for someone else's benefit?

Maybe you're thinking, *Everything would be fine if ________ just got off my back.*

Often someone else is inflicting pressure on us to change, and we can confuse that with *our* motives and values. Other people can lead us to the water with the best of intentions, but they can't make us drink it. That is something to get very clear about before committing to these practices.

The Stages of Change framework, also referred to as the Transtheoretical Model (TTM), 🔎 was developed by James Prochaska and Carlo DiClemente in the late 1970s, as the result of a study examining the experiences of smokers who quit on their own without requiring further treatment—to understand why some people were capable and others weren't.

The model focuses on decision-making at the individual level, operating on the assumption that people don't change behaviors quickly and decisively; rather, habitual change occurs continuously through a cyclical process. This is scientific proof that healing is not linear, verifying and validating that change can be complex and is not instantaneous, so stop beating yourself up for being human.

The Stages of Change are as follows:

- Precontemplation – no intention of changing behavior
- Contemplation – aware a problem exists but no commitment to action
- Preparation – intent on taking action to address the problem
- Action – active modification of behavior
- Maintenance – sustained change; new behavior replaces old
    - (Possibly) Relapse – fall back into old patterns of behavior

At the time I stormed out of Dr. G's office, what stage do you think represents my stage of readiness to make a change?

Did you guess precontemplation?

Ding ding ding! What do we have for them Johnny?!

The precontemplation phase is essentially denial. I had no intention of changing my behavior and I did not see any reason to do so. Where do you think you rate on this scale?

This leads us to another popular framework for enacting health-related changes. The Health Belief Model (HBM) 🔎 was originally formulated in the 1950s by social psychologists working in the U.S. Public Health Service to explain the failure of participation in programs to prevent and detect disease. Since then, it has been expanded upon and adapted to fit diverse cultural and topical contexts. The constructs of this model for this stage of awareness are broken down into three categories: 1.) Individual Perceptions: perceived severity and perceived susceptibility; 2.) Modifying Factors: perceived threats and cues to action; and 3.) Likelihood of Action: perceived barriers, perceived benefits, and self-efficacy. *Self-efficacy*, also known as situation-specific confidence, is a person's belief in their own ability to take action. The Health Belief Model is still used today for disease prevention and health promotion, a classic example being observation of human behavior regarding alcohol consumption.

Applying this framework to my state of mind at the time of my psychiatrist appointment, I did not believe I was susceptible to becoming a full-blown alcoholic, and I certainly did not think my problem was serious enough to warrant any behavior modification, so what was the point of changing anything? Why fix something that I didn't see as broken? Even though there had been numerous examples of how my drinking had become unmanageable, I had to do more "research" and collect more "data" before I became even remotely close to changing my patterns of behavior. Once I did, I had to think about how confident I was in successfully making those changes (self-efficacy).

Spirit Steps

Merging and applying both psychological models, answer the following questions through the lens of your current shift in behavior. Try to be as objective and nonjudgmental as possible.

Read the questions below without filling them out just yet:

How would you rate your willingness to change (1 to 10)? _____
Why? ________________________________

How confident are you in your ability to change (1 to 10)? _____
Why? ________________________________

What challenges and obstacles may arise?

____

What are the consequences of *not* acting?

____

What are the benefits if you are successful?

____

Does your behavior follow any patterns? Is it triggered by certain people, places, or things? Are there certain times, circumstances, seasons that you find you are more likely to engage in these moments? You may want to refer to the previous activity where you charted these connections.

Take a deep breath in through your nose and exhale out the mouth. Sit comfortably and set a timer for five minutes, close your eyes and notice what comes up for you, without holding back. Now, write about this experience and complete the questions above. Be gentle. Start small.

Write down, *I am committed to exploring possible areas for growth as I faithfully embark on and continue this journey.* Then put one hand on your heart and say it out loud, "I am committed to exploring possible areas for growth as I faithfully embark on and continue this journey." Sign your name under the statement to express your dedication.

Congratulations! You are willing to explore your behaviors on a deeper level of self-awareness.

Chew on this section for as long as you need. Repeat the lessons and practices, they are an ongoing part of your journey, not a one-and-done. Revisit this place when your life is weighing too heavily on a particular escape route, or something feels out of control. You aren't the liability; your maladaptive coping mechanisms are the real problem, and they have nothing to do with your true self or your true Spirit. You have a trove of resources to tap into and a source of infinite power at your beck and call. You are not alone. You are loved. You are supported. You are so much more than enough.

Chapter Two
Allow

/əˈlou/ verb
give the necessary time or opportunity for
Allow for new possibilities.

I fought tooth and nail to make things happen my way. I had to become willing to admit that I couldn't do it alone and that maybe someone out there had better ideas than I did. Until this point, I thought that anything other than figuring everything out on my own would have been meek and cowardly. The truth is we can't do this alone because we are not designed that way.

Some refer to this attitude of seeking help as surrendering. That concept can be a tough pill to swallow. As a culture, we exalt and celebrate self-knowledge, reliance, and the increasing value of independence over interdependence. "Surrendering" has come to connote negative themes of weakness, helplessness, giving up, quitting, a country that waves its white flag and begs for mercy. Wipe that image out of your mind. Reframe the notion of surrender as an act of strength, hope, and commitment.

Even if we do not quite know what or to whom we are surrendering, or the exact intricacies of this abstract construct, we are still acknowledging that we cannot handle our problems alone and we are thus inviting help. *Allowing* help.

Moment of Clarity

My dog, an elderly yorkie named Harley, looked up at me from the passenger seat. I used one hand to hold the phone to my ear and the other to flick my cigarette out the window, my knees keeping the steering wheel steady. "I don't even think I'm gonna drink today," I told my boyfriend of the season. "If I do, I'll probably just have one or two beers."

I really meant it.

I knew I was on thin ice. I had already put this guy through so much in the short amount of time we had been together. Cheating on him when drunk. Disrespecting him. Each time, I begged and pleaded for another chance. I promised it would never happen again, and I felt so guilty that I couldn't control my drinking. I didn't know who I was becoming.

I arrived around noon to my grandmother's 90th birthday party at my mom's house in Southern Maryland. I sat alone on the deck looking out at the Chesapeake Bay. *This is easy,* I thought. *I can do this. I'll just drink this bottle of water. Everything is cool.*

A few minutes later, my sister's boyfriend came out to join me on the deck. I watched him casually dig a bottle of beer out of the cooler, shaking off the ice that stuck to his hand. *A beer does sound nice.* I nonchalantly grabbed a bottle of Flying Dog IPA for myself—after all, what's one drink going to matter?

Removing the top with my lighter, I heard the heavenly *pshhh,* as the air released. I let my entire hand get ice cold as my fingers wrapped around the bottle. I brought it to my lips and poured it down. The crispness, the bubbles, the strong bitter taste, the knowing I would feel better in just a few seconds. I could finally breathe. I could let my hair down, put my feet up, and not worry about a thing. I don't remember the second drink much less the third or the fourth, and I surely don't remember the exact number of bottles I went through, but I am certain it was not the innocuous one or two I had promised.

I woke up at home in my bed very confused. Was it the next morning? How did I get back here? I performed the routine search for my wallet and phone. Check. Harley was sleeping soundly next to me. Check. Everything was there. I peeked out the window and squinted through the offensive and intrusive sun (the audacity it had to rise). I saw my car outside, thank God. My head was pounding, so I quickly shut the blinds. But wait, that meant I drove an hour home. On beltways and highways. In a blackout. With my dog in the car. My baby.

Palm to forehead, I walked to the bathroom and looked in the mirror. Frown lines furrowed my face, a roadmap of disaster. I felt possessed. I had been slowly fading and losing my shine but for some reason on this day I saw it more clearly; the image was sharper. I didn't recognize myself. I realized in that one moment the madness that had become my life. It had finally caught up with me, almost like coming to consciousness after a long nightmare. I sensed this woman in the mirror asking, *Who are you anymore? What are you doing with your life?* I didn't answer. I couldn't think of a response that made sense.

For months, my therapist David (another professional I sought under the pressure of another boyfriend), had been gently suggesting that my drinking might be a problem, and that abstinence is typically the only solution for addiction. He recommended that I check out some recovery programs. I scoffed at the proposition, "That sounds great for alcoholics, but my drinking is not the issue. I will never, ever stop drinking altogether." I assured him that I was in therapy for my mental health issues, not my drinking, and that he needed to stay in his lane. Yet week after week he heard stories of my alcohol-driven antics, accidents, crises.

But in this moment, looking in the mirror, out of ideas, and not an excuse left, I silently acknowledged to myself that I wasn't drinking because I wanted to, I was drinking because I needed to, and that was terrifying.

I finally landed in one of those recovery meetings David told me about. On a Saturday morning, I sat in an empty pew of a church and looked at the stage. I purposely chose the outskirts of the audience in case I needed to make a run for it. On the stage sat a middle-aged man with a wide smile. Surrounded by balloons, one plastered with the number twenty-five because he had been sober that many years. I couldn't even fathom it. Why was he *happy* about this?

I am nothing like this man, I thought. *None of these people understand what I am going through. This isn't going to work.* Then I noticed he was wearing slip-on black-and-white checkered Vans, just like me. So, we had at least one thing in common after all. And for some reason that was enough for me to take the meeting halfway seriously. After he spoke for a few minutes about how amazing his life was now that he was sober, others in the audience began to share about their own experiences.

I don't remember a word that was said, or what I absorbed in those sixty minutes. I do know that when I got back into my car, I felt hot. I placed my head in my hands and bawled. I couldn't identify the emotions. I think it may have been a combination of the fear of *Oh shit, I really do have this thing* mixed with the relief that *Oh shit, I really do have this thing.* Because that meant I now knew I could find help which meant I had to stop living this way.

99.9 percent of me still thought I was destined to live a horrible life, that I wasn't a true alcoholic, but there was this tiny .01 percent that entertained the idea, *What if ... I am an alcoholic?* More importantly, *What if I could actually get better?* The thought hit me like a ton of bricks. I hadn't considered that I may actually be able to improve my life. I was scared of trying something new and failing, but deep down I knew I had to at least make an attempt. I was out of ideas for how to figure things out on my own.

After that meeting, I went home, smoked all the weed I physically could, journaled incomprehensible thoughts, and then dumped the rest of the baggie in the toilet. That was on September 5, 2015. Hence, my sober birthday is September 6, 2015.

Something within me, and something without, said *enough is enough*. I finally recognized the utter insanity of my lifestyle and realized that no matter how I spun my stories, unsuccessfully justifying my actions, or how long I sat in my room reading self-help books, a sick brain could not heal a sick brain. Sometimes it takes true desperation to move the needle.

I see this difficult time in my life as a gift. I don't know that I would have sought help had I not sunk this low because on that day, I saw something different in the mirror. I saw complete and utter defeat. Our most painful moments can become catalysts to change and pathways to freedom.

Often, in crazy-making situations—be it a toxic relationship, addiction, or an unhealthy living situation—we experience a moment of clarity amidst the madness. Even if only a blip or glitch, it is enough to ask ourselves, *What in the actual F am I doing?*

Pay attention to these feelings, these windows of clarity. We can choose whether to listen or not, but the Universe will inevitably tug for our attention, usually gently.

Imagine holding onto a rope so tightly that your knuckles turn white and your hands blister, the rest of your body sacrificing all its systems to maintain your strength. Now, imagine letting go. This is what it feels like to relinquish our false sense of control and let in a higher source of help.

One of the ways I like to conceptualize an open attitude and letting go of our pride and ego is through the spirit of willingness. This is one of the most important components of all transformation. Willingness is defined as *readiness* or *the quality or state of being prepared to do something.* Even if we aren't completely ready to ask for help, we can become willing to look at things differently, which is a huge step. Just like my moment of clarity looking in the mirror, this window of willingness may be fleeting, so take advantage when you catch even a glimmer.

This is grace peeking through.

Open Heart

I didn't know if I was capable of getting better. In fact, I thought there was no way in hell, but there was also a tiny part of me whispering, *What if you can?* Even though I didn't understand how that would look, and was scared by the uncertainty, I listened to that part of me.

At first, I was reluctant to trust in something I couldn't comprehend. Humans are very skeptical beings, which benefits us in many situations. There is a reason we evolved in a way that promotes this characteristic; it protects us from harm, from being conned and fooled into something potentially dangerous. But we have become so cynical that it blocks us from delving into the unknown. The best scientists will admit there is far more that we *don't* know about life than we *do* know. Far more that is unseen than seen. Phenomena that can't be explained away by the scientific method, Socratic questioning, or any of the other ways our human minds like to tidily and logically solve problems.

You are reading this book because you have a light in you that wants to be exposed, expressed, and felt. You know there is more out there, and you are right. You don't have it all figured out right now, and the good news is you don't have to. One step at a time.

This is where the T word comes in—Trust.

Are you willing to trust what you may not fully understand?

Let's look at the ways you are likely already trusting in your life, without even knowing it:

Are you not going to board an aircraft because you don't fully understand how flight patterns work, or exactly what goes down in the cockpit, or the systems used by air traffic controllers? You are putting an awful lot of trust into a man-made invention, the pilot, the flight attendants, the engineers, and a 200-ton machine that will soon be going 550 miles per hour at a 35,000-foot altitude. Yet we trust it all and go about our business, relaxing and reading a book until the plane lands safely. Fully surrendering, though not quite understanding how this miracle of transportation across a thousand miles happens in two hours. (But please don't clap when the plane lands. It's weird and annoying and makes others uncomfortable. By "others," I mean me.)

Even if you didn't go to medical school, you still rely on the resources of healthcare, right? We might not fully understand how a doctor heals our broken bones, or comprehend the inner workings of an X-ray machine, or know the way each of the 206 bones in our bodies operate and mechanize with one another, but we sure do trust this expertise when we need it. Without a question.

You get the point.

These are all examples of trusting something outside of yourself.

Receiving

We each have our own histories and relationships with religious deities so saying that the concept of Spirit is a sensitive subject would be an understatement. When I first entered recovery, I had gravitated too far away from the God of my upbringing, and I felt judged. For some reason I interpreted the messaging of my childhood religion as fear-inducing, and I couldn't face the shame. Through a second chance at faith while getting sober, I was taught to develop my own vision of a higher power and consider the exact qualities I wanted them to possess.

Come up with your own ideas about Spirit, force, presence, love, God, maybe even a relative who has passed on or someone you see as a guardian angel. Trust your intuition. Call it the OG if you want. He, she, or they don't care. Language can't capture it anyway. When beginning to embrace this idea of Spirit, I chose Johnny Cash. Johnny wears black and he is just like me. I am not scared of him because he understands me, and he has done it all. When we talk, he has a cigarette in his mouth and laughs, "Oh girl, what'd you get into this time?" Your higher power will evolve throughout your journey and is not a fixed concept. At the end of the day, none of us fully understand what is out there. For the sake of comprehension, I use the terms *Spirit* and *Universe* throughout this book interchangeably.

Spirit Steps

If you could choose someone or something to have on your side, what qualities would you like them to possess?

How do they offer help?

What do they do for you in a crisis?

Can you picture them in your mind's eye?

What do they look like, sound like, feel like?

Do they have a name, gender, occupation?

How do they dress?

Sit in silence for a few minutes and consider how you would like to conceptualize your personal Spirit that is always working for you, conspiring in your favor. Jot down anything that comes to mind and describe this entity.

Release

The cool thing is that when you finally ask for help, the guidance will be ready for you. As if they have been waiting eons for you to call on them. Spirit *wants* to help. You don't have to beg or demand or force or manipulate the Universe. Release your need to control everything. What a relief to learn that you don't have to work so hard to make everything go "right," whatever that means. We are responsible for contributing to the process of self-change, but we aren't in control of it. This Spirit entity is working with you, so think of your connection based on collaboration and co-creation rather than a relationship of subservience.

What if you lived in a way that demonstrated a deep trust in the Universe conspiring for you?

It is useless to think of this critical step of allowing Spirit to enter as a defeat just because it involves a certain degree of humility. We are simply admitting that there is only so much we can control and thank goodness, because many problems are far too big for us to put in a tidy box and check off the list. Humility is also a form of self-acceptance, which is critical to making change. This gives you the power of choice and the power to act. Accept where you are today and express a willingness to be open to new possibilities, and perhaps a new source of energy will hold your hand in the process. Just as we take advantage of airlines to travel and hospitals to heal, let's also consider using Spirit as a resource we can rely on, regardless of whether we are able to fathom its limitless influence.

Oneness / Unity

"No man is an island, entire of itself; every man is a piece of the continent, a part of the main."
-John Donne

Spirit resides in every one of us and thus we are all connected. By seeing life as anything other than that, and holding onto this rigid individuality and uniqueness, we separate ourselves from Spirit. We are so much more alike than we are different. We are here to help each other, and the Universe speaks through other people.

Many of us were raised with a suck-it-up attitude. *Wipe your brow and continue, no matter what. Don't show emotions. Don't talk about your problems.* I interpreted this as a requirement to be perfect all the time. On top of the fact that perfection is an illusion and only leaves you feeling worse, it also blocks you off from everyone and everything else. The first person in my family I talked to about my alcoholism was my sister. She became someone I went to for support. At first, this felt so foreign to us because our conversations had always been very surface level. But something interesting happened once I started sharing my feelings with her. *She* started sharing *her own* feelings and I learned more about my sister in several months than I had known our whole lives. We are now best friends, and I can't imagine not having her to lean on. This never would have happened if I hadn't let her in.

We aren't on this earth to isolate from one another. No matter how much we try to separate ourselves—claiming our possessions, property, and established mental concepts, also known as our egos—we are all made of the same stuff. Instead of dividing and exiling ourselves, why not take advantage of this great vastness and shared infinite power to connect and grow together?

Whatever you believe to be the reason we are all here—Nature, a Creator, the Universe, God, science—the important thing is to recognize this entity as bigger than you. It is a miracle to be alive and you are *supposed* to be here, at this time, in this location, the exact way that you naturally exist.

You hold within you the same spark that dwells in the Spirit. You are in essence, a creator yourself and a magical being with infinite power. Claim your power. Don't hide from it.

I am eternally perturbed when I see this popular catchphrase plastered on mugs and totes:
"I am enough."

Enough is "Did I put *enough* sugar in the recipe?"
Enough is an adequate amount of something.
Who set the bar so low?
"I am enough."
Enough for what?
You are *so* much more than enough.

Spirit Steps

Where did you get the idea that you aren't enough?
Can you identify these thoughts or trace them back anywhere?
Close your eyes and take some deep breaths. Set a timer for five minutes and see what comes up. Jot down your findings.

You must protect and strengthen the light within you. Keep the spark lit, nurture it, and see how it comes to imbue your being.

Let Go, Rinse, Repeat

Surrendering is not a one-and-done process. It requires diligence and devotion, as well as self-efficacy and an unwavering faith to move through the appropriate steps toward a solution. You must not only trust the Universe, but also that inner voice of your highest self. As you begin to fine-tune your intuitive skills, this will become easier and feel more natural.

The best outcomes unfold when I allow and trust rather than when I orchestrate, force, and control. We are very good at the latter methods. We are taught to excel in logical and rational thinking, and we value those qualities. We learn how to manipulate situations to fit our desires and expectations. Because we are good at *do*ing. The harder task is simply *be*ing. So, we have to continuously practice letting go.

I thought that the process of recovery from drugs and alcohol would be its own escape route, albeit a healthy one, to discard all my problems and shut the door on my past. I was wrong. Recovery was just the beginning, the base of the pyramid to my growth. At first it was very uncomfortable. Everything felt so real and raw. There was no longer a cloud between me and the rest of the world, no longer a cloud between me and myself. I have hit multiple moments in my life where I had to re-surrender in big ways and fall on my knees once again crying, *I need help. I don't know what to do.* And then there are the more subtle times of surrender when I can't find a parking spot or don't understand why the grocery line is taking so long.

Give Yourself Permission

You don't have to wait until you hit the proverbial rock bottom. You may just be feeling emotionally unaligned, or your soul has gone dark, or you want to make your life better. If you feel that your situation is worsening and that the elevator is only plunging further downward, closer and closer to the bottom, just remember you can get off at any floor.

An attitude of willingness and surrender is a life-long development, no matter how much we think we have learned or how spiritual we believe we have become. We must always remain teachable. This in and of itself becomes a discipline to be cultivated.

Spirit Steps

Starting tomorrow morning, write down in your journal, "I am open to the concept of Spirit. I am looking forward to what it will show me today." Write this as many times as you need throughout the day. Close your eyes and say it to yourself out loud or silently. Know that you can come back to this openness and state of receiving whenever you wish. Pay attention to what happens when you enlist this help.

Once I surrendered and allowed help into my life, I had to figure out why I was using alcohol in the first place and what purpose it served. A scary question, but with this foundation of infinite support and wisdom, I had the strength to take necessary actions on the road of self-exploration. Now that you have this inner power and greater access to Spirit, you are ready to dive into the deeper work.

Chapter Three
Shed

/SHed/ verb
to eject, slough off, or lose as part of the normal processes of life
In Autumn, the trees *shed* their leaves.

A large chunk of self-discovery is about *un*learning. Peeling away the layers of conditioning by our culture, family, and other areas of influence that have hardened our exoskeletons, to see what lies beneath.

"Can you remember who you were before the world told you who you should be?" If this question, posed by poet and novelist Charles Bukowski, makes you uncomfortable it may be because you know deep down that the way you're living does not match your true core values—before you learned from society what you *should* value.

This disconnect is called *cognitive dissonance.* 🔎 It describes the mental anguish we experience when our true feelings and beliefs don't align with our everyday actions and behavior. Most of the decisions in our lives have been made *for* us and not *by* us. Once I understood this, I saw I had been reading a script someone else wrote. Once this seed was planted, I slowly decided to become the director of my own life. It didn't happen overnight; a lot needed to shed before I could grow into myself.

I call this process shedding because I believe one of the classic misconstructions of the transformation movement is that we are trying to become something new, making ourselves into someone else, "new year, new me," "change your life in thirty days," etc. But it is more so a returning to who we are, a remembrance rather than a brand-new start. A renewal. We got a little lost somewhere along the line and are now stripping away what doesn't fit to make space for our true Spirit.

Band-Aids over Bullet Holes

When we don't have a clear sense of self, we look to others to show us who to be—systems, people, places, ideas, movements. We want to feel a cohesive identity and purpose, but our self-concepts have been compromised with issues (often originating in childhood), such as neglect, abandonment, feeling unseen and unheard, or mental and physical abuse. Never having been properly treated, these injuries fester and become infected. We blot at our spiritual and emotional wounds with gauze and patch them up with cheap medical tape and Band-Aids because they are too gruesome to look at. We seek out the wrong partners for an instant fix. We obsess about the newest handheld device that will solve all our problems. We sleep for days to numb out and escape from it all because the wounds are too painful to face.

We constantly seek solutions OUTside of us to make our INsides feel better. I used drugs and alcohol, looked for attention and validation in all the wrong places, restricted my food intake, intensely focused on my visual appearance, and a host of other tactics to protect my wounds from surfacing. We aren't crazy or weak-willed or forever flawed for engaging in these behaviors. We have human emotions, and we react to thoughts and feelings differently. This is natural and it is not your fault. *However*, as you are now reading these words and acquiring the knowledge and ability to practice self-awareness, it *is* your responsibility to become willing to open your mind, make room for changes to your inner space, and develop the skills to rewire yourself accordingly. We let ourselves bleed and then we grow.

YOU are the *only* one who can truly fulfill your needs and heal these wounds, but you aren't alone in this process. You can utilize your Higher Source and support system. When we heal from within, we reclaim our power to choose our actions wisely and with conscious intention. It becomes easier to identify and release what no longer serves our Soul. Thus begins the shedding process.

Be a Snake

Snakes shed their skin four to twelve times a year, a process called *ecdysis*. You may have seen images of their dead sheath lying lifeless nearby. Before snakes let go of that outer shell, a new layer is already forming underneath. Just prior to shedding, the snake's skin begins to turn bluish and its eyes become opaque, hindering its vision.

Sound familiar?

Periods of intense growth can feel disorienting. Like snakes, humans become confused and unsettled during life's transitions before we can successfully move onward to the next phase. Finally realizing the old ways aren't working, we blindly grope for new methods to function, new ideas to formulate, but we don't know where to go next.

A snake's new skin cannot emerge until the old one is shed. Just as we experience growing pains from shedding tired behaviors and thought patterns, it is uncomfortable for snakes to rid themselves of their outer layers. But this process helps them in the long run by removing parasites and other unhealthy matter, in the same way that we let go of components of our systems that have been bugged by unhealthy mechanisms and maladaptive patterns that insidiously and gradually poison us—gambling, smoking, overeating, unhealthy relationships, the list goes on.

In contrast to the snake's very natural and instinctive process, we humans must make a more intentional choice. We shed the most harmful layers first. The ones with the most imminent and lethal of parasites. In no way, shape, or form could I focus on my true identity while drowning myself with alcohol and drugs

I simply could not and would not face reality.

Until I had to.

The internal conflict of getting sober, the inability to imagine my life without alcohol but knowing I couldn't continue that way, was treacherous. I was caught in the middle of my old life of recklessness and chaos versus the new life of uncovering my buried soul. One foot in each world, I was lost in the chasm between the two. These jumping off points can feel insurmountable. Like we are going crazy. Utter insanity.

But this space, the confusion, the in-between, is where the magic happens. This moment of uncertainty is when the possibility of the unknown starts calling to us; new insights begin to form. We reorient ourselves as we gain the faculties and clarity we need to take the right route for our Spirit. We trust that the new skin is forming underneath even if we can't see it happening. We must glide by faith, not sight. Like the snake, we are growing. Like the snake, we are shedding skin. Like the snake, we are moving onward to the next phase.

I got sober and cleaned up my life. Part of this was as simple as cleaning up my act in the most literal sense.

Your Outer Space Reflects Your Inner Space

I used to love coming home at the end of the day and putting on my red double XL *Scarface* T-shirt. It was my "hangover shirt" throughout my Lost Years and it signified that the whole day would be spent in bed. I wasn't drinking anymore, but I was holding onto the sloth energy of defeat, resignation, and demoralization. It wasn't only clothing I had to pitch—random stuff, trash, tchotchkes, papers, pictures. Things I had been hanging onto for no reason, lacking awareness of the energetic attachments they had on me.

My life needed a makeover.

I started paying more attention to the clothes I wore, taking pride in my appearance, putting on a touch of makeup even if it was just to run errands. I completely upended my living space and got rid of 80 percent of my belongings. Clearing my physical surroundings helped to clear my mind. My desk stayed organized. My bed stayed made. I started to feel better, act better, and live better.

The places we spend most of our time are often paid the least amount of attention, because few people (if anyone at all) see them. Really, this is all the more reason to design these personal areas exactly to *your* liking. A place you feel safe and free, where you can breathe and create and flow and relax and reflect and grow. As we shed negative thoughts and beliefs, we begin to shed the physical things around us in tandem. Both the seen and unseen will naturally slip away and fade out. Don't overanalyze or get stuck on this. The Universe is conspiring for you, not against you. Change is good. Change is necessary.

Spirit Steps

For some prompting, refer to the cues to action below:
Sit on the floor of your favorite room (perhaps on a pillow).
Squirm around, get out all the fidgets.
Then, settle in and make yourself comfortable.
Relax your jaw and all the muscles in your face, then the muscles in the rest of your body.
Close your eyes and take a few deep breaths, in through the nose and out through the mouth.
Soften into the space.
Blink your eyes to open and look around the room. A slow, turning, peripheral view of the 360 degrees of space around you.
What catches your attention?
How do you feel looking at what surrounds you?
Name the thoughts and feelings.
What would you change?
Make one significant and reasonable change and see how the energy shifts.

Under the Surface

As things started to get a little more real day by day, I learned that there were less obvious auxiliary factors to address that ran deeper than my physical space, and that my escape route of drinking was only a symptom of underlying issues. Several vices were contributing to the unmanageability of my life, impeding any chance of growth or change.

Some were more apparent than others—facing and accepting that I had been diagnosed with bipolar disorder at age eighteen. Some were more subtle—distracting myself with intimate relationships to affirm my identity and validate my worth. I could easily walk into a bar and receive shallow instant gratification, but as my head and heart started to clear up and my conscience returned, the emptiness of that lifestyle became palpable and cognitive dissonance unbearable. I stopped dating completely, and no longer sought attention in unfulfilling places. I didn't have enough headspace to worry about a guy when I didn't even know myself. I chose character-building over comfort. This was so painful and lonely because I wasn't really a fan of me.

Subtle Foes

Everything in your life, every person, place, or thing either supports your journey or detracts from it. Yes, there are gray areas here and there. Yes, the waters can be murky, but usually it is pretty obvious. Sometimes it isn't the thing or person itself, but your relationship with it or them that needs shifting. This is an ongoing process that becomes more intuitive and refined as time goes on. These phases are interlinked, and you will see this come up again in the Stabilize part of your journey when we discuss how to protect your energy and establish boundaries as part of maintaining an even keel.

Spirit Steps

What is weighing you down, holding you back? What constrains your energy and keeps you from becoming more alive? Each time you shed a layer, you add energy to your life because you are revealing hidden pieces of yourself that were imprisoned and suffocated by all these skins. What in your life is no longer serving you? Look at the following categories and consider what is not resonating with you—what/who you no longer relate to, what you want to let go. As you read, you might want to jot down a few notes and see where this takes you.

- Habits (escape routes, denial, over-indulgence, health-compromising behaviors)
  - What feels out of control?
- Things (materials, clothing, presents, mementos)
  - What occupies your mind and causes stress?
    - What do you want that you are scared of not getting?
    - What do you have that you are scared of losing?
- People (the nature of your relationships)
  - What boundaries can you set?
- Ideas /beliefs /assumptions
  - Which thoughts are hindering your progress?

Be gentle with yourself. There can be a grieving in this process. Some of these layers of "skin" have been with us for so long we feel it is actually part of our inherent beings.

Acceptance

As we peel back the layers, we drill down to the core of who we really are. The word acceptance often connotes acquiescence or giving in to a less than desirable situation. But acceptance is not resignation. We are simply acknowledging that this is how things are right now. At the same time, we understand there are changes to be made. We accept both of these truths in tandem.

Unconditional acceptance is the bedrock to discovering our most authentic nature.

You do not need to hate the skin you are currently in.

These layers have been working hard to protect you.

All of them have served a critical purpose in your survival.

Of course I am shameful about my drinking, the awful decisions I made during my Lost Years and the people I hurt, but I also accept that alcohol made my life more bearable at a time when I felt hopeless to the point of contemplating suicide. It got me through difficult days, months, and years.

This highlights one of the fascinating ways that humans and animals are different. Snakes don't sit in shame, dwelling on how they attracted certain parasites or why a layer of skin no longer fits. It is counter-productive and further delays growth. You will be fighting yourself. Fighting nature. This cycle of self-loathing will cause you to unnecessarily dwell on the negative.

Some common ways we question ourselves to the point of stagnancy and paralysis:

Why am I this way to begin with?

I will never be able to change.

What's the point?

This is just who I am.

Sound familiar? This is the attitude of defeat rather than acceptance. If you keep up such negative and helpless narratives, you will continue to live that way. The Universe will match your energy.

You must accept yourself unconditionally right now in this moment, no matter the layers—this is not just to say the physical skin but also the proverbial skin we have been discussing—flaws and all. Throughout my Lost Years, self-love was a foreign concept. I honestly could not wrap my mind around even liking myself, but acceptance felt a little softer and easier to digest.

"The curious paradox is that when I accept myself just the way I am, then I can change."
-Carl Rogers

Acceptance does not come over night, sometimes you must first act *as if* you accept yourself. Consider, *What would a confident person do here? What would someone I look up to do?* Then do that. After all, we are very good actors. We have spent our lives reading a collectively and culturally curated script.

You are right where you are supposed to be, in the natural part of your cycle. Everything you have ever gone through—good, bad, dark, light, hard, easy, simple, complex, shallow, deep—has led you to this place, to this skin you are in. Feel appreciation in this moment because that attitude will move you closer to reading the real script—the one that reflects you and only you.

To thine own self be true.

Let Go

Beginning the shedding process is the initiation of self-discovery. It may be scary and painful, but it is necessary; after all, just like the snake, your growth has already been happening underneath. What you are letting go is also letting go of you.

Do not be so stuck in your ways that you can't shift with the world around you or the world within you. Let your imagination run wild, let your growth take you on a new route, even if you don't quite know where it's leading. Don't be so fixed in your ways that you can't allow new possibilities and fresh awareness to enter. Before I embarked on my healing journey, I thought I was a bad person who was beyond redemption. I had lost all hope and had nothing to look forward to. I warned people not to let me in their lives because I was a natural disaster. I would tornado into others' orbits and cause complete chaos, all the while looking for anything or anyone else to blame. But I realized that wasn't who I really am. I was just lost. Once I started letting bad habits shed, I started operating more naturally. I finally stepped away, got out of my head, detached, loosened up, and viewed life from a different perspective.

Let your body and your soul go through ecdysis. Slough off that old skin and leave it in the past. Let it become part of the earth again—those clothes don't fit your Spirit anymore; they don't fit you anymore.

Be like a snake:

Bend and glide.

Flex and contract.

Shed what no longer serves you.

Stay alert, vigilant, agile, strategic, versatile.

Accept yourself.

Then let yourself shine and slither more effortlessly.

Stronger than ever before.

Chapter Four
Unlock

/ən'läk/*f* verb
undo the lock of (something), access the full functionality or data
Self-inquiry encourages people to *unlock* their hidden potential.

Shedding or ShRedding?

I'd love to say that one day I woke up and decided to become a healthy, responsible, contributing member of society. The truth is, I experienced the "gift" of desperation. I had been diagnosed with bipolar disorder at age eighteen as an inpatient at a medical recovery center for anorexia. Ten years later, I would be hospitalized again, this time for a major depressive episode and suicidal ideation—a fancy, clinical way to say that I no longer wanted to live. I didn't want to make my friends and family sad but at the same time I didn't understand why it wasn't *my* choice. Why couldn't they just "let" me die, by giving me a pill or shooting something into my veins. Schlepping into one more day felt unconscionable. Life was too painful, and no one knew how it felt to live mine. Didn't they want what was best for their daughter, sister, friend?

It turned out, the Universe had a different plan for me. If I wanted to do anything meaningful with my life, I had to face and accept the reality of my mental health. I knew self-discovery wasn't an optional, new hobby to take on for fun. It was necessary to carry out this critical mission with which I was entrusted. It was necessary to stay alive. So, I set out on the road less traveled and started to get real with myself. This process was slow and steady.

The Scientific Method of Self-Inquiry

Whether we are aware of it or not, we conduct experiments every day. We act, receive a reaction, and then base our next action on said reaction. Perhaps as a toddler you could get whatever you wanted by pouting and stomping your feet. Years later, with your first high school boyfriend, out of mere habit, you use the same tactic. He breaks up with you. You are left feeling devastated.

Notice how short and tidy that paragraph is. If this were real life, we would have ten pages scrawled down about why our partner acted a certain way, the evidence of self-victimization, the unfairness of it all, but when you look at a situation objectively, the personal nuances are placed aside. You can get down to the actual nuts and bolts of what is going on and the next right action to take. These findings then inform your future decisions around that behavior.

Experiments are bred from curiosity and seeking. Motivation to fill a gap in understanding, to see things from a new perspective. The best scientists stay neutral and open-minded, regardless of their emotions or affinity for their hypotheses. The data must remain unbiased to maintain integrity. Especially in the early stages, investigators don't jump to conclusions or let emotions lead them astray. Likewise, you don't need to form any hard-and-fast opinions or judgments about yourself, or rush to interpret the results. You are simply gathering the raw data to be sorted and later analyzed. Some emotions might crop up and we note them as we go, we don't deny them, but we don't dig deep into each one and set up camp. We zoom back out to the purpose of the experiment. As in the first phase where we discussed raising awareness, at this point we are simply Noticing.

In this experiment, you are a discrete entity, while also considering all the external conditions that have shaped you. As individuals, we must take responsibility for creating and deciding our own unique meaning of life.

So much of our lives is spent in autopilot, as if we have been programmed by social pressure. We walk around in conformity, like automatons coded to eat, sleep, work, and repeat. We continue to operate from that standpoint until something in our outer or inner world changes. Until a bug appears in the program—dis-ease, restlessness, anxiety—and we can't figure out what went awry or why the wires got crossed.

This "bug" is where the experiment begins.

Lab Rats

In our hustle culture, speed is highly valued. Where are we going? We don't know but we want to get there as fast as we can! We are busy people, and to be busy means to be important, and to be important means to be successful. Right?

Researchers and scientists use rats in their laboratories because rodent behavior mimics human behavior. Just as rodents spin around those little wheels for exercise, we repeat the same behaviors cursorily. The illusion of movement disguises the fact that we are only going in circles and ending up nowhere. Up until my late twenties, I was very active in this race. I was committed to winning. Yet every afternoon, I experienced the same feeling of darkness, dread, and defeat as I drove home from work, wondering if this would really be my life for the next however many years.

I didn't know where the finish line was or what I was going to win once I got there (maybe a trophy?). It didn't make sense, but I still steadily climbed the career ladder, promotion after promotion. Slowly and painfully, I learned that ladder was propped against the wrong wall. With a heightened sense of awareness in sobriety, unable to drink or smoke or self-sabotage my pain away, the misalignment grew more unsettling as the days passed. I felt hollow inside—a shell of a person without any heart or backbone. But I still begrudgingly kept on with the race.

"Running away from one's problems is probably the most futile thing in the whole world, for the simple reason that all your problems are really in your own consciousness and, your consciousness being the essential You, it is not possible to run from it."
-Emmet Fox

Just as one can't run forever, you can't live in cognitive dissonance forever (and why would you want to?). Though I couldn't quite identify the bug—where it lived inside me, its origins, or how to get rid of it—my body and soul knew something was off. I had spent my whole life feeling that I was on a completely different wavelength than everyone else, so I tried to fix it by attempting to fit into a space that wasn't my true shape. I had to be perfect so that no one would suspect I was a fraud. By trying to keep up with the masses, I was living in a state of anxiety and anguish, reciting my lines and playing my part. The subtle hints hadn't been enough to motivate me to change. I was so frustrated by my lack of contentment. Everyone else seemed to be doing just fine. Was there a manual for life on earth that I had failed to be given?

In 2016, on a cold December night following the holiday season, I laid on the floor of my bedroom writhing and crying inconsolably. I couldn't pinpoint what was wrong. Life seemed meaningless and I just wanted to escape from it all. Escape from myself.

My sister and therapist arranged for me to be taken to the hospital where I would stay for ten days, followed by several months of outpatient treatment. Through art therapy and other healing modalities, it became clear that I could no longer read from that misfitting antiquated script. In fact, I had to change the whole play and production, the scenery, the plot.

I see now that this episode was a blessing. My break*down* led to a break*through*. Emotions are to be honored and respected, not shoved down as we have been accustomed. Viktor Frankl, Holocaust survivor and author of *Man's Search for Meaning,* wrote, "A man's concern, or even his despair, over the worthwhileness of life is an existential distress but by no means a mental disease." So many of us struggle with a deep feeling of purposelessness, guised as clinical behavioral health issues. Thus, the discomfort is tranquilized by treating the symptom rather than getting down to the root cause of suffering. We constantly pacify these signals when we should be investigating what is setting off the alarms. It's not so much a disease that needs to be treated, as an entry point to growth and self-discovery that deserves to be acknowledged.

Down to the Core

Despite the armor of arrogance I wore in an effort to keep it all together, I knew my exterior could disintegrate at the slightest poke. Since childhood, I have been told that I am "too sensitive," a trait that doesn't bode well in the fast-paced environment of a capitalistic, success-driven, dog-eat-dog society. This discomfort and shame caused me to turn toward anything that might "free" my mind and "ease" my worries, and in turn numb my soul.

I always considered myself flawed for feeling so much, seeing my sensitivity as a liability. Now I see that our emotions are guideposts, indicators of pain that need to be explored, of patterns that need to be interrupted, of stories that need to be told. Feelings are blessings—data that can be used to implement healthier conditions to produce better outcomes. I had to remove things, add things, and tinker with this and that, a lot of trial and error.

As I stripped away the layers of maladaptive coping mechanisms that had been repressing my truth, I discovered that the frantic rigmarole of the rat race is not conducive to my health or my performance. The speed of hustle culture just doesn't work for me. I now aim to navigate this world in ways and at a pace that honor my core values and unique perspectives. Even though some moments are excruciating, and at times I don't know how I will make it, I do know that I will make it. I know that through the processes of Shed and Unlock, I allow a clearer and stronger and truer me to emerge. Today, I am grateful for my ability to feel so deeply because this strength gives others permission to do the same. To live fully, truly, and unapologetically. To me there is no greater gift.

Variables

Repeating the same experiment over and over and expecting a new outcome is pointless, crazy-making, and to be honest, life-sucking. If nothing changes, nothing changes. All scientific studies have limitations and room for error, and humans are no different. You may have to practice a lifestyle shift several times before trusting the results.

When we try something new, we are simply adjusting the variables. The word "variable" comes from "vary"—implying room for range and fluctuation. Testing out new ideas doesn't mean committing to something forever. Nothing is etched in stone. We are simply observing patterns and implementing alternative variations. I had to relearn what I like to do, who I enjoy spending time with, and how I want to live my life.

Sensory Experiences

Ten years ago, when I first tried to alter my cigarette-smoking patterns, the e-cigarette didn't work for me. I missed flicking the ash, the smell of real smoke, exhaling out of my car window, leaving the bar to go outside with the smokers, my hoodie smelling like cigarettes. All these visceral sensations sustained my addiction.

Now, I see that certain sensory experiences can also incite *positive* behavior patterns. Being mindful of the way my yoga mat feels under my feet, the sound of meditative music, the sweat dripping into my eyes, the after-class shower washing away the grime and grit. Tactile motion, space, surroundings—all of it can be so sensual. Paying attention to what you hear, taste, see, smell, feel, in the moment is powerful and this becomes the ritual. We learn what we like or don't like by being present to and accepting each experience as it comes and goes. Fully tuning in and raising awareness. Noticing.

You look forward to these repeated moments because they are part of your safe space. Even if everything else is going crazy in your life, you know this one thing will be consistent, three times a week (or whatever you decide). Wear that headband you love or buy a special water bottle to use just for this practice. Almost like a Pavlovian response, hearing the people around you breathe in and out to let you know what's coming, making it both a familiar space and a brand-new exploration each time.

Rituals don't have to be dogmatic. Routines offer structure, while some actions fly free. Find a fun balance and learn what works for you personally. It's like a dance. It doesn't have to be perfect. Spontaneity can do wonders. We will learn to apply and finetune rituals in the next chapter Stabilize, staying aware of what works and what doesn't. Always come back to your "why" to help you stay on track. Realize how this behavior change fits in with the rest of your life rather than obsessing about the outcome.

Aim to see every day as a new set of data to collect. Get excited about it—This is your life! Be thankful you have the ability to see through a new lens of inquiry and curiosity.

Spirit Steps

Consider and reflect:

Which moments in my day leave me feeling peaceful yet energized?

- Calm yet courageous?

Which moments leave me feeling aligned?

Where do I find meaning?

What do I like?

What do I not like?

Who do I want to spend time with?

Are there any relationships that feel like an obligation?

Pay attention to how you answer these, and what cues the body and mind proffer. You might realize you spend a lot of time on something that you don't really enjoy, it zaps your energy and gives you a headache; or perhaps you associate with a person whose presence continually makes you anxious.

As you get acquainted with who you are, you will begin to Notice that life is asking questions, and you will be held responsible for answering. In doing so, you will slowly start to dial in to your own place in the Universe. Your coordinates. Picture an optometrist swinging the lenses and clicking them into place, asking, "Which is clearer? One or two? Three or four?" As you inch closer and closer to your redefined prescription, you determine your best vision, perspective, and proprioception for successful navigation of the world around you.

You don't have to have everything (or anything) figured out and perfected before you try something new. This is a common struggle for recovering perfectionists (*awkwardly raises hand*). *I must earn more degrees, receive more certifications, practice a wider variety of spiritual principles.*

Stop the excuses.

Just go. Try a variable. If it works, take note. If it doesn't work, take note just the same. You are the scientist. Will you take on this project? Will you say Yes to your life? Because if it's not a Yes, it's a No.

It's All about the UN

No, I don't mean the United Nations.

The "un" words: Unlock, Undo, Unlearn, Uncover, Unleash, Untame, Unveil.

We must loosen our grip on beliefs we have clung to that we let define us and determine our every move. Unleash your true self. What is underneath all those layers you are shedding? Love, awareness, peace, harmony, unity, nonjudgment. That is true of every human being. What differs is how we express and channel that power.

As the real me began to emerge, what I once saw as loneliness shifted to a serene solitude and deep appreciation for my true self. I started to enjoy my own company. I learned what works and what doesn't, that I am an introvert and need a lot of time in introspection, time to sit outside the land of the living, forming thoughts and integrating insights to interpret the world around me.

Remembrance

When you start acquainting yourself with your innermost being, it becomes increasingly difficult to engage in behaviors that oppose, mask, or deny this purity. We didn't become programmed in one day and we are not going to be *de*programmed in one day. We must pull the pieces apart and sort through them. We need to dissect the system.

The "bug"—old ideas and philosophies—will continue to crop up because we have been living in hypnosis for a long time. We must rewire ourselves in a way that doesn't feed the bug, but instead strengthens the anti-virus software to overpower the damage caused by old ways of being.

This old way of being was an interference, not your true self. You aren't embarking on a "new me" project. You aren't becoming a different person out of thin air. You are remembering who you truly are, believing what you innately know, and embodying the truths that have been covered and muddled along the way. I will be the first to admit that I'm not proud of many aspects of my past, but that shame won't be the hill I die on. I am not a bad person. I was lost and sick. You might be feeling similarly, to a degree.

The good news is that it's never too late to return. It's never too late to wake up. And wake up you must because you are the only one who can do life the way *you* do it. You cannot be replaced, nor repeated. You are the only one who holds the true essence of you-ness, and your mission is important. The world needs YOU.

To stay in this space of remembrance and celebration of our true selves, we must constantly remind ourselves how we got here, and how we may continue operating from this standpoint, to live in harmony with ourselves and our highest purpose. The faulty program will always be there, swimming around, doing whatever it can to lure you back in. It will flash shiny things and tantalizing chemicals and present wolves in sheep's clothing to tempt you, especially in times of transition as we grieve our old selves and reconnect with Truth.

One practical way to rewire is to identify our thoughts and where they come from so that we may alter them to accommodate our revised schema.

Here is a real-life example:

Event: I received an email from the chair of my department saying she wants to meet with me about the course I taught last semester.

Automatic Thought: *I must have done something wrong. I knew I was too late grading my students' papers. I shouldn't even be teaching. They're going to learn that I'm not good at it. I'm probably in so much trouble.*

The "old" me would have been fearful, needing to know right away exactly why my superior wants to talk to me. The me I now strive to be changes the thought to: *I have no idea why she wants to meet, which means it might not be a bad thing. If it is, I will learn my lesson, which will make me a better professor in the long run.*

After that conversation with myself, I emailed her that I was looking forward to catching up. I even asked if she would be on campus the next day so we could meet in person. I took the opposite action instead of choosing fear and avoiding or prolonging the issue.

It turned out the "issue" was completely made up by the bug in my brain. She wanted to know how the students received the material because she was considering changing the curriculum. It had nothing to do with me. Many of our worries, I would venture to say the majority, end up never happening, or they are in the past and there is nothing *to* do. These counterproductive thoughts rob us of the present moment. If we aren't here now, we are nowhere.

When you start to get in a tizzy, put your automatic thoughts aside and ask if you are being tricked into thinking everything isn't okay. Look around. Where are these problems? Essentially, we are figuring out healthier and more reasonable ways to view tough situations. Because there will always be tough situations and there will always be tricky thoughts associated. We can't control them, but we can improve how we deal with them, depending on the quality and state of our inner space. This method is an example of how we might reframe delusional thinking into a realistic and helpful alternative.

Once we have the data on what works for our souls, we develop and implement systems to keep us on track. Maintenance. As we undo the no-longer-useful, outdated programming, we figure out how to spend our time and energy. When sailing uncharted waters through deep self-exploration, it is necessary to keep the faith and remain curious and open to the unseen, to the unknown, the uncertain. If we stay devoted to our practices and trust that the Universe is conspiring for us, we can build patterns that last. We can stay with ourselves. With little actions and subtle shifts that build up over time, we can remember who we are and expand our power.

Chapter Five
Stabilize

/stā-bə-ˌlīz/ verb
to make stable—steadfast or firm
He began to *stabilize* and was able to reach a state of peace.

A great deal of patience and faith are needed to enact and sustain subtle behavior shifts, trust the process, and give it time and space to work. Repetition is needed to successfully implement these habits. Referring to the Stages of Change model in Notice, this is the *maintenance phase*.

A new course of action may seem easy to *begin*, but more difficult to persist as old thoughts and behaviors interfere. Conceptualize this as constructing systems that facilitate new patterns rather than a solely goal-oriented approach. We have all attempted health or diet challenges that have only lasted a few days. Sometimes staying is even harder than starting. Staying in the room, staying in the yoga pose, staying in the emotion, staying in the moment, staying the course, staying devoted to Truth, rather than letting decoy thoughts misguide you. This is the only way to break the spell and reverse the fear-based hypnosis that has become your reality. Stay-bilize.

There will be obstacles and setbacks and temptations thrown your way. You must continually remind yourself *why* you are taking this path. Why are you committing to yourself? Instead of trying to see where you can squeeze healing time into your day, build your schedule around these habits and systems. Respect this sacred space for yourself. By grounding and recentering, our focus increases and this balance makes the rest of the day run more smoothly and efficiently. Knowing when to stay is just as important as knowing when to go. We stay in the moment to receive the right direction and guidance from our inner wisdom and Spirit, which will tell us when to leave a situation if appropriate.

Protect Your Energy

Balancing your mental and emotional states must be your number one priority.

Without that, we are building our lives on quicksand. This is especially important for those of us who are highly sensitive and deeply affected by external stimuli and environmental features. We learn how to shield ourselves while maintaining the ability to appropriately interact with the world. This delicate flow is acquired and fine-tuned as we practice it more and more.

Everyone needs a team of wisely chosen people in your corner. 🔎

We all have purpose, whether we realize it or not. Who do we want with us on the journey? My own team is comprised of my therapist, psychiatrist, family, friends, recovery mentor, and other healers across various modalities. I am the employer and they each play an important job and function in my life. I keep them on the payroll, and they keep me on theirs. This "payroll" is our exchange of energy, how much time and resources we invest in one another. We learn to Shed certain parts of our inner and outer lives and this isn't a one-and-done process, but rather an ongoing refinement that happens as we get to know ourselves better and align with our true purpose.

There are likely people in your life you didn't choose to employ, but they hover on the periphery by default—family members, teachers, colleagues, associates, and other social connections. In the large organization of life, not everyone is under our management, and we still must deal with them. Notwithstanding, we don't have to talk to them for hours at the water cooler, greatly delaying our important tasks and becoming resentful. We can set boundaries and manage our expectations.

Take stock of the company you keep. Spend time with healthy people who have what you want and who encourage you on your journey. Some aspects of your lifestyle may need to change if *you* want to change. When you are surrounded by people who shame personal growth, their narrative will become yours. You will live according to their scripts and start following their example. Put more simply, if you hang out with barbers long enough, eventually you're going to get a haircut.

Stop trying to get apples from a lemon tree. There may be something you want from a certain person in your life. Perhaps you always wanted a good relationship with your brother, but he constantly interrupts you when you're sharing your feelings. Time and time again, you get upset about this. You aren't mad at your brother, you're mad because you have certain expectations that are not being met and you continue to look for this care in the wrong place. You're mad because you are doing the same thing over and over and expecting a different result.

Be real with yourself. Find out who you can rely on based on the degree of severity, emotionality, and intensity of a situation. Figure out who on your team is right for the job and will best handle the energy exchange. Even though you didn't hire some of the people in your lives, and may not be able to fire them completely, you are still in charge of the payroll. This is where your power lies.

Intimate Relationships

Your partner is your co-collaborator. They support you—your purpose, your projects, your endeavors—without hindering, complicating, delaying, or confusing progress. In essence, they cause more beneficence than harm. I know emotions run high in this area and it is not so black and white, but sometimes we do have to step back and look at a situation objectively. This section will surely trigger some. I have been there, and I understand the sensitivity around this topic. It can feel like an attack. But this is also why I am so passionate about it. We receive false messaging that we must stay in relationships and work harder and stick in there no matter what. These feelings and unhealthy attachments can be confusing, counterproductive, and misleading.

Yes, self-exploration can occur while in an intimate partnership. People do it every day. But if you are on the fence about that person, and it's not obvious whether they will support you on this journey, if it's not a *hell yes*, then it's a clear no. Ask yourself, would you still be with this person if you knew from this day forward they would stay exactly how they are at this moment? Or are you waiting for them to get their act together so they can be there for you? There is no guarantee of change or that it would be enough even if they did show some progress. You can't afford to gamble here. It is a high-risk bid, and the odds are not in your favor. This isn't a Blackjack table in Vegas. It's your life. Your energy. Your worth.

"But he's really working on things and trying to be better."

I hear this all the time. If he truly is, that's great. Only you can decide if it's enough to warrant a spot on your roster for the assignment at hand. If you're thinking you can fix him, let me tell you that it's hard enough to stay devoted to your own transformation, much less trying to control a person over which you have absolutely no control.

"But, but, but…"

I know this game far too well. I made all the excuses in the book. Until I told myself: No. Enough. Picture your life one year from now, will you still be saying, "But?" How about ten years from now?

If you still don't know the right move, then stick around to collect more data. That may be the appropriate action at present, and it's a great starting point. You will know when it is time to go. Do I sound uncompassionate? That is the big illusion. We often think we are helping someone by holding on tightly, by being their hero, playing the martyr, when in reality both parties are being harmed.

My ex-boyfriend's manipulation, dishonesty, and emotional abuse left me in a state of exhaustion and incoherence. I started questioning my reality, my sanity. A fight-or-flight state had become the norm. Ultimately, I had to choose my sanity and wellbeing over our relationship because it put me in such an extreme deficit. It wore me down. I had to set him free. Anyone who impacts you so deeply on an energetic plane, down to your nervous system, will have a ripple effect on the rest of your life, weakening your sense of self, dimming your light, and certainly diminishing your soul.

Trust your inner voice. If you betray it and stop listening, you will lose connection, you will lose yourself, and that is your one true love, as Spirit is at our core.

The moral of the story is that even if you try to mediate and reason with this member of your "team," sometimes it's not enough. I recruited the help of detox programs, rehabs, and therapists in my attempts to rehabilitate my relationship. But I lost so much over the course of those two years that I just couldn't keep him on the books anymore. The return on investment (ROI) was no longer calculable. He was complicating my mission, and it was crushing me. His intentions were good, he was just very sick and couldn't play well on the team. His actions and behavior didn't just affect *me*, they affected my whole network of support—sometimes directly, more often indirectly.

Just as we are the boss of our own lives, other people are the bosses of theirs and you may be cut from someone else's roster. Just because you no longer align with another's path, that doesn't mean there is something wrong with you. Let them go. The relationship ran its course and that's okay. Trust when these separations happen. Even if they are painful, these are necessary openings on your road to truth, light, and ultimately love.

Alone = All One

Balancing relationships with personal growth can be difficult, hence much of this inner exploration and discovery must be undertaken alone. Many of us are scared to be by ourselves. That's okay. Sit in it anyway. Choose character building over avoiding discomfort. If you are paying attention to and tending your inner space, your external reality will start to reflect those rewards.

The definition of alone is "having no one else present." Somewhere along the way we began interpreting this as something negative or shameful. The prefix *al* means "all." If we break the word down to its components, we see its deeper meaning is "all one." Although we may be by ourselves physically, we are still connecting with the power of oneness and unity in humanity. At our deepest seat of Self, we all carry that love, nonjudgment, and pure awareness. Being alone is an opportunity to merge with Spirit.

The word "alignment" also shares the same prefix. All in one line, arranged in appropriate positions. When we are in states of alignment, we have more agency over the stories we tell ourselves and can channel the forces that drive our daily decisions. We aren't relying on external influences to determine our worth.

You and Spirit can become one. *All one.*

The Narrator

If you were narrating your life, scene by scene, how would the story go?

For years, I told myself I was damaged beyond repair, too mentally ill to function, a natural disaster. So that is what I continued to do. Changing the tune can be extremely difficult. If your behavior isn't matching your standards, you either have to alter the behavior or change the standards. I chose to lower the standards and diminish my values. When I was faced with the opportunity to get well, I had to start telling a more hopeful story, which meant taking the opposite action. I had to keep telling myself this upgraded story over and over for it to become the new script.

If you were reading a story to a child every night, what would you fill their brain with? Horror and monsters and fear? Or hope and strength and empowerment? If we are constantly worrying about how we *don't* want our lives to end up, we aren't making space for our true destiny, which is always the better ending.

The victor tells the story, and you are the hero of your journey.

Spirit Steps

If nothing changes, nothing changes.

What can you do today that your future self will thank you for?

To answer that question, you need to have some idea of that "future self," the soul you are re-embodying. You need to remember your why.

Imagine your life one year from now.

- Who is around you?
- What are you doing?
- What have you accomplished in the past few months?
- How do you feel?

Take a moment to consider these questions.

Close your eyes and envision this iteration of your future.

Transport yourself through time and let anything and everything come to the surface.

Reflect on the mental and emotional state of achievement, the overall vibration.

Living with a clearer mind, a more comfortable body, amplified energy, whatever the case may be.

Embrace this feeling as if you already have it, picture it in your mind's eye, see yourself embodying it.

While in this heightened state, think about your "why."

> Why is change so important to you? Keep asking why and drill down. *Why do I want to lose weight? To look better. Why do I want to look better? To find a date. Why do I want to find a*

date? Because I don't want to be alone. Why don't I want to be alone...

When there is no rhyme or reason, no passion, no *why*, it can be difficult to stay the course. Figure out what is standing in the way between here and there, between now and then. Only you are.

A manifesto is a published declaration of intentions, motives, or views. Based on what you gleaned from your vision practice, write down what is coming to you in the future and then act as if it already exists because it does, you just haven't received it yet. Write the manifesto in present tense. Make it a page long.

Here are some excerpts from my personal manifestos, as you can see, anything goes!

- I love my career. I travel around the world showing and teaching others how to live authentically, freeing themselves from old patterns and limitations.
- I feel comfortable in my body. I am active and healthy.
- I have friends who love me and need me.
- I live simply and abundantly.
- My creativity heals myself and others.

Your "Why"

This is where behavior change begins. We start with the vision, figure out how our "why" aligns with our self-concept and values, and then break the big picture down into manageable pieces.

Subtle shifts. Practical lifestyle modifications.

Stay dedicated to small steps, to the present moment. You can't boil the ocean, so come up with commitments that are sustainable and realistic. Habit change and transformation do not have to be a punitive endeavor. Lose the archaic precept that the prize is only rewarded or deserved through hard work and suffering. Dispel the notion that pain and grind and self-abuse are necessary for true accomplishment.

What if success could be easier, dare I say… enjoyable *and* healthy?

All our stories are different, especially when it comes to healing, returning to Self, and aligning with the Universe. There is no one-size-fits-all plan. I personally like to monitor and record my habits and behaviors because 1.) Putting pen to paper organizes my brain and 2.) The mere act of self-observation affects the behavior.

You do not need to be rigid. We are aiming to get away from damaging and harmful patterns.

Don't we have enough rules in our lives?

Smart watches track our steps. We count days on a calendar. Water bottles measure our sips. Phone apps calculate our calories. Measurements. Metrics. While benchmarks, objectives, and frameworks may be helpful, the rigidity and counting can start to feel obsessive and taxing. You know yourself and whether that will limit progress. Maybe you know that you need those hard and fast rules to stick to it, and that's fine. Stay honest and self-aware. Have flexibility when your "system" needs to be tweaked.

When we aim for perfection and fall short by eating one cookie, when we swore we would eat none, it's easy to throw in the towel and eat *all* the cookies because we convince ourselves that "all hope is lost." We tend to live in these extremes of dichotomic and distorted thinking. However, if we are gentler, objectively taking note of why we didn't hit our target, that information can be used to develop different strategies so that we can operate more effectively the next time, just as we do in the Notice phase of raising awareness and then practicing those strategies when we Unlock our true selves.

Build a Practical Routine

"How we spend our days is, of course, how we spend our lives. What we do with this hour, and that one, is what we are doing. A schedule defends from chaos and whim. It is a net for catching days."
-Annie Dillard

The personal time you set aside is about connection—to your Self and your higher power. As if you are in an old-fashioned call center where the operators all sat in one room, phones ringing off the hook. All the voices around you muddling what you hear from your own receiver. By making your inner voice louder, the volume of external chatter decreases by default, so the message for *you* can be heard the clearest. So that you can Allow in your true Spirit. You can't lower the volume of the world, but you can bring your own voice into focus.

Consistency is everything. Simply carving out this container for yourself is a big move toward attracting what you want in your life. You are sending a clear message to the Universe,

"I am committed to growth. I take my mission seriously." Routines and rituals give you freedom, not restriction.

Believe it or not, these habits will become a safe space for you. All forms of ritual have physical and psychological features, the combination of which show evidence of better emotional regulation. Thus, the act of simply engaging in a ritual, no matter what it is, can have psychosocial benefits.

Even if it seems that everything in your life is going crazy and all the plates are spinning at once, you know there will be at least one point in your day they will stop and you can breathe and come back to your safe space. Allow for impromptu moments. Rituals don't have to be dogmatic; they offer structure and anchors so that you can fly free in the areas that matter most. Find a fun balance and learn what works for you personally. It doesn't have to be flawless. Keep tweaking your practices and consider what works and what doesn't. After all, this is part of the overall experiment. We are simply collecting data to inform our actions.

When you wake up, take stock of your morning routine. Don't change anything, just observe your behavior. Be honest with yourself. Are you reaching for your ~~pacifier~~—whoops, I mean cell phone—as soon as you wake up so you can start scrolling Instagram and TikTok and checking on your Amazon delivery? How long are you spending there? Nothing you are doing is bad or wrong, you are just witnessing patterns, practicing the tools you learned in the Notice phase, and seeing if perhaps some tweaks might improve your daily outcomes.

Let's say you scrolled your phone for ten minutes. Tomorrow, try to not reach for the pacifier right away. (Life hack: Investing in an alarm clock is one of the best decisions I have ever made. My phone does not have to sleep next to me. It has its own bed. Just as I need to limit my screen time, my phone needs to limit its “Lindsey time.”) Dedicate that same block of time you would normally spend on your phone to something different. Start there and work with that.

Try the Spirit Steps below for two weeks. If you hate them, you never have to do it again. If you miss a day, fine, get back on track the next. Life isn’t about learning how to never mess up, it is about course-correcting and snapping back into alignment. Try all of them or two of them or one of them, it is up to you. The goal of this activity is not perfection. It is a way to expose you to a buffet of healing modalities to see if any resonate with you.

Spirit Steps

Implementing rituals and changing habit patterns takes practice, and you have permission to make the rules for your own life. You are the main character. Simply setting up this space for yourself and getting clear on your intentions will have benefits in the short-term and the long-term as you clarify your vision.

On the following pages are five clinically proven morning steps that have worked for me personally, to increase productivity and enhance wellbeing.

Morning Mix[2]

Step 1: Cleanse

When you first open your eyes, put pen to paper. Allow whatever comes up. This is called open stream of consciousness. It could be your dreams, your grocery list, your plan for the day, that funny joke you want to tell your sister, the list of reasons your boyfriend is pissing you off. If you're still staring at a blank page, write about how you have nothing to write about and the feelings associated. Dump out whatever is up there onto the page and take this moment to cleanse the mind before you start the day.

This is also a great opportunity to set some intentions that are personal to you. These can be quotes, mantras, affirmations, wishes. By energetically getting on board with your desires, they will enter your reality. Focus on what you want to happen, not on what you don't want. When we worry, we are planning for something bad to happen.

Some of my favorites:

- Today the Universe will show me my next step.
- I pay attention to each present moment and accept it exactly the way it unfolds.
- I am open to signs and synchronicity.
- Every day I get to know my true self more and I love myself unconditionally just as I am.
- Thank you, Spirit, for telling me what I need to know.

---

[2] If you already have a morning routine and don't look at your phone right away, that's wonderful. You can still read along and see if any of these practices might contribute to your existing rituals.

By writing our intentions,[3] we are affirming what we already know to be true—even if our heads have become clouded with lies and distortions.

Step 2: Awaken 🔎

Wake up and get the juices flowing. Sit up and start to gently move your body. Roll your head from side to side to loosen your neck. Twist left and right to open the spine. Do a full body stretch, pressing your fingers and toes in opposite directions, lengthening all your muscles. Get out of bed, stand up straight and reach towards the sky as your gaze follows. Bend your knees slightly, gently fold forward, and let the top of your body hang heavy over your legs. Shake your head yes and no. Let gravity do the work and let go of your upper body. Slowly rise and bring your hands to your heart.

Step 3: Breathe 🔎

Standing or sitting, close your eyes and take a clearing breath in through your nose and out through your mouth. Inhale for a count of three, hold the breath in for a count of three, exhale for a count of three, and hold the breath out for a count of three. Do at least three rounds of this breath work. If you feel that you want to stay with this breath pattern longer, go with it.

Step 4: Ask 🔎

---

[3]I won't go into depth on manifesting but a great place to start is by purchasing the guided journal from 369project.com and/or reading the book *Ask and it is Given: Learning to Manifest Your Desires* by Esther Hicks.

Situate yourself however is comfortable and close your eyes. Let your mind wander. Observe your thoughts. Ask the Universe questions. Think back to Allow and your concept of a higher power. Some people call this praying, I like to call it asking. You are requesting guidance for your next step, and to be shown the way through your day.

Step 5: Listen 🔎

Motionlessness seems to be the most difficult practice for most people. Understandably so. We are always focused on doing rather than being. You might be thinking, *But my mind goes crazy, I have too many thoughts that come up. I can't focus*. This is exactly why we sit still and listen. To calm the mind. Saying your brain is too active to sit in silence is like insisting you're too dirty to take a bath.

If you think you don't have time to be still or that your internal chatter is too loud and confusing, that is an indicator that it would very much behoove you to engage in this type of practice. You can always turn your attention to your breath as a helpful anchor.

I know, it's scary. Sometimes my mind feels like a pinball machine—racing thoughts slamming into the sides of my skull. Each thought has a life of its own and they tend to be in conflict. They are animals and your brain is their den. Sit with the lions and watch them. Don't play with them, don't try to fight them off, don't try to hide and run away from them. They won't kill you. Treat the lions like cubs, creatures who don't know any better. You are not the cubs; you are observing them from a place of impartiality. Over time, simple observation will naturally quiet them down 🔎. Facing your thoughts will take away their power and influence.

Some thoughts are like an itch, and the more you try not to scratch the itchier it feels. You are in a state of resistance, which gives your thoughts more authority and more control. Satisfy the itch. Minimize it. Let it be heard and then let it go.

Eventually, you will have the power to softly and non-judgmentally guide them. When a negative thought comes up, *I am a loser and will never have what I want in life*. Whoa, whoa, whoa, slow down Simba. You don't know that. I'm not going to get on board with that one, sorry. How about, *I am in a place of open-mindedness and exploration to bettering my life*.

This time to yourself in the morning can be as structured or unstructured as you want. Try journaling for five minutes, asking for one minute, and so forth. Some people like to be fluid, others prefer to set a timer. These were very uncomfortable practices for me at first. I had to set a timer to know that it was eventually going to end. I had not looked inward in a long time, and never to this degree. The word fear often connotes external imagery—fear of spiders or snakes or heights, but I believe what goes on inside can be far scarier. Be gentle on yourself.

These "rituals" may feel strange at first. Eventually, they become natural, until they are embedded in our brains and we can override the negative thoughts and habits. And don't you dare start judging yourself. You're trying to make your life better, and you are brave for opening your mind and having some semblance of faith that it will work.

You are on the right path.

Trust it.

Evening Ease

Unplug. Put your phone and other screens away. TikTok will still be there in the morning, and your phone will be fully charged! I've had phone conversations at night that I regret because I was too tired to think straight and the part of my brain that helps regulate my emotions had already been asleep for hours. These miscommunications would not have happened if I had put my phone away at a reasonable time. Of course, not everyone has the luxury of going completely off the grid. People have kids and sick parents, and they need their phones on hand at in case of emergencies. That's fine. You don't have to put it all the way on silent. Maybe just plug it in away from your bed, and if it rings, go to it… the old-fashioned way.

Celebrate Small Victories

Once you start realizing what you are capable of, you build *self-efficacy*—an individual's belief in their capacity to act in the ways necessary to reach specific goals—also referred to as situation-specific confidence. *Since I did that breathing practice, maybe I can try for another small change in my morning.* Having the requisite knowledge to perform a task is one thing, and the conviction that you can successfully carry out the behavior is another. Eventually, nothing seems out of reach. Because nothing is out of reach. You are limitless. You do one little thing and then another and another and another and you start to feel a little better than yesterday until the days add up and you feel a lot better.

Remind yourself how certain behavior changes fit your vision. Instead of obsessing about the outcome, notice what is going on in your body as you engage in the practices you choose to implement (movement, writing, meditation). Pay attention to how you feel in the smaller moments of victory rather than casting such a long net and losing yourself in the faraway future. How is this behavior serving you *today*? The benefit may lie in empowerment, knowing you are making changes. Trust yourself and your abilities.

When you feel lost, envision the future version of your highest self. Praise yourself for taking intentional action every day. As you start to believe in yourself, realizing that *you can do it*, self-efficacy will be the fuel that helps you stay on track, or course-correct when you find yourself veering away. No matter what, stay devoted to yourself.

Coming up next, we will learn how our soul can become more deeply involved at a practical level, and how to trust that we are living in alignment and how to act accordingly. With wonder and bravery.

Chapter Six
Leap

/lēp/ verb
jump or spring a long way, to a great height, or with great force
I will *leap* across the threshold.

"Um, hey. So, I don't know how to drive on the left side of the road," I tried to sound chill on the phone, to not express my palpable anxiety. I was embarrassed to call Marissa, the only person I knew on the island, because I realized we had only ever emailed and texted. Since St. Croix is a U.S. territory, it hadn't occurred to me that the road situation would be any different than on the mainland.

She responded in a way that didn't make me feel stupid, "Oh, okay, yeah, so what someone told me was to always keep your elbow in the ditch," Marissa said calmly. I was relieved she was sympathetic to my dilemma. "So literally stick your elbow out the window and make sure you are always on that side of the road so that your elbow is in the ditch."

I was scared but what else was I going to do? This wasn't a place with Uber. I rolled my window down with the manual crank and let the hot air fill the car as I bent my arm and stuck my elbow out. Pulling out of the airport parking lot, I saw a horse being ridden bareback on the main road. Now, *that's* not something you see at Reagan National on the George Washington Parkway. I headed to Christiansted, the main "city" on the island to meet Marissa and her boyfriend, Tanner.

I parked as soon as I found a spot and set off on foot for the intersection where she said they would pick me up. My new flip phone, part of my attempt to disconnect with the modern world of overwhelm, was no help for navigation. I felt panicked walking on the unnamed narrow one-way roads. Apparently, signage was optional. I texted Marissa: "I don't know if I'm in the right place, but I'm wearing a lime green t-shirt and crazy pants." After a few minutes she spotted me on the corner of the road, and I literally hopped into her and her boyfriend Tanner's olive-green jeep. No doors, no top, and basically the bare minimum structure needed to hold an automobile together. It was awesome and it felt so natural to be there. Rolling hills wound us in and out of the edges of the North Shore, looking over the Caribbean.

Tanner pulled the jeep into the sand in front of a beach bar appropriately named Freedom City. I felt intimidated by the guys and girls around me carrying their standup paddleboards—participants of the "Coconut Cup" competition—while I ate my waffle fries. I walked down to the edge of the water and let the sea run over the tops of my feet and through my toes. I suddenly felt self-conscious in my yoga pants that were every color of the rainbow. I wondered if I was equipped to live such a life—could I ever be that cool and free-spirited?

The next night, I sat at a bar called Angry Nate's in Christiansted, read my book and sipped on my seltzer and lime, picking at a veggie burger. I overheard the bartender talking to a guy who said he was just checking out some places and doing some traveling here and there. Once she made her way over to me for some casual conversation, I explained my story which was similar. She introduced me to Bradley across the bar and said we were both there for the same reason and should hang out. I had already noticed him sitting by himself and pegged him as a tourist. Not only did I pick up on his Boston accent, his crew haircut, clean-cut appearance, and sense of seriousness didn't fit in with the locals. I sat next to him, and we chatted. Only a few years older, he too felt lost. He explained that he had been working as a cop in Boston for seven years and felt completely empty and bored with his life.

Interesting that I too had been at my government job for almost seven years exactly. We sat on the boardwalk, watching the seaplanes glide onto the water for landing, and then as it got darker, fireworks began. The deep-fried smells from the food stands wafted towards our bench. The audience crowded together as bodies clothed in shiny sequined outfits danced around us and between us, their decorated eyes glittered and drops of sweat sparkled as their faces caught the light.

Apparently, this was a celebration for Transfer Day Centennial, the 100th anniversary of St. Croix being purchased by the United States from the Danish for $25 million. What a time to visit, neither of us had any idea. We went to a few different bars and met some island people. I remember one man laughing, "Yeah, I came here for a visit ten years ago and I can't seem to find the airport to get back." It didn't seem weird to be here or to move here. It was completely normal to all these expats. They seemed happy. A different spirit shone through them.

Bradley and I walked around, and he asked what I was doing the next day.

"Oh! I'm going to yoga in the morning, you should come," I offered enthusiastically.

He laughed, "What are you doing after that?"

"I don't know, I wanted to head out west, but the GPS in my rental car isn't working."

"I wanted to go west too but I don't have a car."

"Well, I think we can make a good team. I have a car, and you have a map. Let's go west tomorrow."

"Sounds good but I'm not going to *yog-er*," he said, with his thick Boston accent.

The next morning, I saw him walking up the hill to my Airbnb. He looked cute in his bro tank that I would normally find obnoxious. I was impressed that he was on time—I wasn't sure if it was the alcohol making his plans last night. Out west we drove. We heard that a bar called Rhythms was the place to go. We played cornhole, met a guy with a dog playing in the water, and then sat at the bar for lunch and chatted with those around us.

I had only been in St. Croix for a few days, but I already loved it. We got to know some locals while we ate, and I explained that I wanted to move there but I didn't know if I could actually do it. A lady at the bar, round with happiness and an *I don't give a F* attitude, looked me right in the eye and said, "You can. Do it before you change your mind. You're thinking clearly right now, once you get back home it will be harder to make that choice." I knew what she meant, that I would get sucked back into the entrapments and the fears and the false security of living in the safety net of the suburbs. It felt like she was channeling a message from a higher source.

The next day, I woke up at 3:30 AM to drive to the eastern tip of the island, and of United States territory altogether. I would be the first person in the whole country to see the sun rise. My feet dangled off the wall of the cliff and I listened to the waves lapping on the shore. Noticing every star in the sky, I patiently waited.

Once the light began to enter the sky and I watched a beautiful progression of calming colors amongst the peaceful landscape, a feeling washed over me. Maybe this was how Cinderella felt when her fairy godmother cast her wand, and she watched as her rags turn into a beautiful flowing ball gown. A wave moved through me. *You are going to move here.* Complete sureness. *That's that.* My next thought was, *I can't wait for my dog to see this place.* I knew I was doing it, the rest would just be details and logistics. I inhaled and let out a deep sigh. My life was about to change.

A few hours later, laying on the bed in the tiny room of my Airbnb, I called my sister.

"Jackie—" was all I said.

"You're moving there, aren't you?"

"Yes, I am." There was sadness in my voice. I didn't want to leave her. We were living together, and she is my best friend. It was a big step outside my comfort zone, outside my *everything* zone.

Now that I had tasted serenity, I didn't want to leave.

At the airport in Charlotte for my layover on the way home, I felt like I was being steamrolled by travelers and their luggage. The speed was overwhelming after living in slow motion for a few days. Stern faces and quick paces blew all around me. It was too much. I closed my eyes, took a deep breath in and out, and sat down in one of the tall rocking chairs. I pulled out my laptop. Before I realized what was happening, I had booked a flight back to St. Croix. I looked at the bold navy-blue letters that popped up on the screen:

Your itinerary for your upcoming trip:
Take-off July 4, 2017, 8:00 AM
BWI (Baltimore/Washington International Airport)
to STX (Henry E. Rohlsen Airport)

My Independence Day. I did it. I had a one-way ticket to St. Croix in the Virgin Islands and three months to figure out the rest.

A shift happened in the moment I booked that flight. I became a path finder instead of a path follower. I wasn't struck by lightning nor a groundbreaking epiphany. The work had been happening behind the scenes for some time. We can't go from rock-bottom to surging full force toward a major life transition. When I first surrendered to a higher power and admitted I couldn't control my drinking, I didn't suddenly decide, *I should move to St. Croix*. I wasn't thinking about moving anywhere. I was just trying to get through the day. This point of awakening happened after I had a year and a half of sobriety and self-discovery under my belt, but it had probably been set in motion years before that, as I faced many obstacles along the way.

In other words, I needed to build a strong foundation and steady structure from which to leap before I could take on such a powerful "soul risk."

Leaping Toward vs. Fleeing From

"Twenty years from now you will be more disappointed by the things you didn't do than by the ones you did."
-Mark Twain

It's important to distinguish between escape routes and a leap of this nature. Some might argue that I was running away from my problems, albeit through a more creative diversion. This couldn't be further from the truth. Pain had pushed me into action, but then the vision *pulled* me to that vital surrender. I had to walk through my anxiety and fear to learn that my "soul goal" had to be rooted in fulfilling my mission.

A major relocation cannot be undertaken in hopes of a geographical cure. If you are looking at it that way, you're just trying to appease your ego. This will not get you any further than an unhealthy vice or escape route would. Wherever you go, there you are. Make sure it isn't only the current undesirable circumstances motivating your decisions. If you are contemplating a move, know that it cannot be an escape hatch masked as a spiritual leap. It must be an intentional place you are journeying *toward.*

You don't need to move to an island to take a leap. There is a big difference between risk taking and risk making. Whether it's a life-altering decision or an artistic pursuit, soul risks respond to one's innermost thoughts and feelings and often involve stepping into the unknown and redefining your identity. Soul risks can be big or small, internal or external. The outcome may be personal or spiritual. Self-reflection, guidance, courage, and staying true to yourself are strongly advised.

I would be remiss to ignore the influence of my privilege in the decision to make this leap. I had been fortunate enough to work for the federal government for seven years which gave me access to top-tier health insurance for mental health treatment and I had some savings built up to fall back on. However, privileged or not, it still felt risky and came with fear and reluctance.

Once you are on the path, the steps will become more natural and things will fall into place as you are drawn forward. When I made the leap to move to St. Croix, it felt like I was manifesting a dream while it was manifesting me at the same time, and eventually we were speaking the same language. It didn't feel like I was *doing* all this, rather it was being *done* to me. Truly.

Direction, Signs, and Synchronicity

Though our external environment may change or shift, the inward quest is more primary than any physical endeavor, so the cues and directions must be followed carefully. We know there is no destination, and it is more about the journey, so if this is true then all the little steps really matter. Do not underestimate the subtle shifts; they add up to the leap. Every move is getting you either closer to or farther from your end game.

If you follow a compass, one little degree will change the overall route. At first this difference is trivial. After one foot you will only miss your target by 0.2 inches. No big deal. After a mile, that discrepancy is 92.2 feet. If you are trying to get from San Francisco to Washington, D.C., one degree off the original starting point will land you on the other side of Baltimore, 42.6 miles away. But we don't have to veer so far off track. We have the power to course correct.

We can learn how to discern whether we are acting on our intuition—the gentle nudges and whispers that come when we are in a state of serenity—or the loud buzzing alarm in our head that makes us feel frantic, signaling the need to eat a full sleeve of Thin Mints or call that ex-boyfriend when we *know* deep down it's *not* the right thing to do.

It takes practice to distinguish between the two. Sometimes anxiety gives us a bodily sensation that might be confused with our gut feelings. Sometimes the signs may surface through pain, warning you that a relationship must end, or that your job has run its course. The more open and willing we remain in sensing these signs and following their guidance, the more we notice them. Eventually, it will become second nature because you are in flow with the Universe. Trust that Spirit is supporting you and leading you in the right direction.

While in outpatient treatment for depression, my art therapy teacher instructed that we create a collage of images that felt like home. Once complete, I realized all my images showed quiet spaces embodying sanctuary and refuge—the forest, beaches, cabins in the mountains. I decided in that moment that, if I truly was devoted to getting better, I needed to find a new habitat.

Maybe this is how birds feel when it's time to migrate. The first time they travel, they're still learning the ropes. They fly in the correct direction according to Earth's magnetic field, but they don't know how far the journey will be. Like a Boy Scout with only a compass, birds use cues from the sun and the stars, until they become comfortable and trusting enough to put their abilities into gear. Although my brain was nowhere close to the instinctual intelligence or precision of a bird, I felt a cosmic force guiding me. My desire to relocate couldn't be explained in logical terms. In fact, there was hardly any logic behind it at all. Yet it was the most character-building experience of my life; exactly what my soul needed at that time. I have learned that our choice of home shifts throughout our lives and is not limited to the nuclear family or a physical location. Home may be a feeling, a memory, an energy, a person, a passion.

How did I land on St. Croix? Well, I knew I wanted to move somewhere with a slower pace, so I asked the Universe for a sign. Over the course of that next week, I heard a few of the other people in my outpatient mental health program talking about vacations they had taken to the Virgin Islands. They named a few destinations, one of them being St. Croix. It stood out because I hadn't heard of it. That weekend, I went to brunch in DC with a friend. I felt so tense, and I told her how the crowds and loud noises were getting to me and that I wanted to move somewhere calmer. Laughing, she blurted out, "Well, you could just move to St. Croix like my friend Marissa and meditate every day." And that was that. I had heard this mystery place named twice within a few days, and I took that as my sign.

This was a "circumstance that appeared meaningfully related yet lacked a causal connection." Carl Jung's definition of *synchronicity*. 🔎 Those moments when something might at first seem coincidental, but also somehow divinely arranged and intentioned. If I wrote about the synchronicities I have experienced in my life since learning what that meant, and even looking back and connecting certain historical dots, my list would be pages long. It is a very powerful phenomenon. Every morning this week, write in your journal or say out loud, "I am open to synchronicity."

Start paying attention to signs and do something one degree in the right direction of your vision. One degree toward what you are seeking. You will begin to pick up on signals and indicators that will gently nudge you in a certain direction, maybe only a few degrees over from your current positioning.

Faith and Gratitude

Skepticism and synchronicity do not get along. Nor does thanklessness fit into this picture. Instead of the typical "I'll believe it when I see it" approach, from which we tend to operate due to our logical brains and our affinity to the scientific method, we must instead take on the attitude of "I'll see it when I believe it." This is faith. Pure faith.

It's scary. Of course, it is. That's why we stay in harmful situations for so long. They are familiar. We become comfortable with our discomfort, knowing all too well that there could be a better world on the other side of change. That there could be ease on the other side of effort. For most of my life, misery was my comfort zone. I knew what it felt like, so I would gravitate back to it like a security blanket. Often, the notions of success and happiness are unknown and thus far scarier.

A major component of keeping this faith and staying open to guidance and suggestions is gratitude. Gratitude is an important ingredient in the phase of Leaping. Consider an employee who wants a job promotion. He works hard, gets there early, stays late. He does all the things. But he has a bad attitude. Every time he meets with his boss, he complains about the hassles of the job, everything that is not being provided to him, the lack of resources, how he works so much harder than the rest of his colleagues. If you were the boss, would this attitude incentivize you to enact change to meet your employee's demands? How would you feel come promotion time about electing this person for a higher position?

Now, consider another person at the same company. When she meets with you, her boss, she conveys how thankful she is to have a stable job. How her vision is expanding on what the company is capable of and that she would love to demonstrate more accountability and help brainstorm processes to improve workflow efficiency. The employee is interested in her personal growth and the growth of the company. To whom would you offer the promotion, if you were in the boss's shoes?

Apply that same thinking to your life. Are you focusing on all that is going wrong and what you are lacking? Then that is what will expand. That negativity is what you will get more of.

Or are you living in a mind frame of abundance, brimming with appreciation for all you have been gifted? Understanding that gratitude will expand and bring even more greatness to your world?

Shift your attitude. Find the coping mechanisms to do so. Do whatever you need to show the Universe, the Creator, whatever name you give it, that you appreciate this life, and that you are on board with operating at a higher frequency and serving as a change agent for the ultimate good of the collective. Become a willing and eager participant in the big picture. This is the launching pad that gives us the courage to be bold. We accept and value our life as it is and acknowledge the evidence that we are already being held and supported. We realize we had the strength to leap all along.

The Non-Linearity of Change

Here, the cyclical nature of change shines its light. We continue to witness and observe our habits from a non-evaluative standpoint, just as we did in previous chapters. Our self-efficacy, situation-specific confidence, increases. It is at this stage especially that we are called to rely on faith, a variant of empowerment that helps us build the strength to achieve our goals and live our purpose. The more we successfully act and follow through on set-out objectives, we begin to trust our abilities and feel inspired to take more risks, again proving the importance of self-efficacy in behavior change.

Identifying cues to action that motivate this leap is helpful, even if those nudges and indicators are mostly internal or signals from the natural flow of life. A cue could be as simple as a Post-it note stuck to your bathroom mirror with an inspirational quote, or a photo of you as a child to encourage self-compassion. We already know the Universe will support us; all we need to do is jump. If we don't, we will never know what beauty is waiting for us out yonder.

Influence and Regret

We will face obstacles and barriers along the way. I don't mention this to attract them into our lives, but to prepare ourselves so we do not become wiped out by hurdles and derailed by side shows. A major deterrent is listening to others' unhelpful and discouraging opinions of your intended leap or soul risk. This is not their path. It's yours.

Because of my history of mental health struggles, I don't always trust my decisions. My therapist and psychiatrist were initially hesitant because they didn't fully understand my motives, but they eventually became very supportive. My father, on the other hand, needed some convincing. He was not happy—because he loves me and was worried. Like any parent who wants to protect their child, he warned me of what could go wrong and questioned how I would tackle certain barriers, such as money to live and the unsafety of being on my own.

I eventually had to tell him—as well as my logical, brilliant, entrepreneur-minded twin brothers—that their opinions had been heard, and I was going to do this with or without their support. If they wanted to help me with the move and logistics, that would be very much appreciated, but I did not want to hear anything that would deter my trip. In other words, the "why" is more important to me than the "how." When I let my soul lead the way, then my brain will get on board to orchestrate the day-to-day practicalities. Too often we get overwhelmed with answering, "*How* will I do this?" before even giving the "*Why* am I doing this?" a chance to make its case. My family, the amazing beings that they are, rose to the occasion and helped me every single step of the way; my brother even flew down with me when I moved to the island to help me get settled in. The Universe assists us with the "how," as it is our collaborator in every soul risk we take.

I also had to get used to what I have now coined the "American eye roll." I see this look any time I choose something that does not fit the conventional path toward success. I know that the industrial system works for a lot of people who live happy, abundant lives, but it did not fit me. I couldn't get on board with grinding for forty hours a week, white knuckling it until the weekend when I could finally let loose and drink myself into oblivion, checking the calendar each year to see which holidays fell on a Friday so that I could revel in those sacred three-day-weekends. I couldn't continue living this way, grueling over my desk another thirty to forty years until I could finally retire and enjoy my days. I didn't want to live a life I was constantly trying to escape.

Memento Mori translates to "Remember you must die." My friends' faces become disfigured with disgust when I say this. Who wants to think about death? The skulls adorning my clothing and accessories are reminders to live life fully, but they can be off-putting to other people. We tend to compartmentalize death as if it will never happen to us, but I think about it often. It drives me to consider the present moment and live intentionally and purposefully.

We listen to songs and read poems about what people decide to do if they know they have only a short time left to live—a month, a week, days— "live like they are dying." But why aren't we already using the time we have been so graciously issued to do what we want? Do we really need a terminal illness or near-death experience as an excuse to finally start living?

Bronnie Ware, a writer and motivational speaker who worked in hospice facilities and other palliative care settings, spent precious moments with the dying—consoling, listening, acquiring wisdom, and providing her love. She journaled about her experiences and wrote *The Top Five Regrets of the Dying: A Life Transformed by the Dearly Departed,* based on her anecdotal research of the trends and patterns she observed in her patients' testimonies. Do you want to know the most common, number one regret from which the other four stem?

"I wish I had the courage to live a life true to myself, not the life others expected of me."

Pay attention to the signs and synchronicities as they come. Observe them, work with them, lean into the flow of life. You are amid a sea change of form, perspective, and depth. What is coming for you, to you, through you, is nothing short of a miracle.

Chapter Seven
Evolve

/i-ˈvälv/ verb
to gradually become clearer or more detailed
Her soul continues to *evolve* over time.

On every hero's journey, there comes rebirth and transformation. There is an essence about you that can't quite be named. This essence is the true you, in all your beautiful you-ness. That is your superpower. The things that make you different or weird are also what make you stand out—your unique fingerprint. One-of-a-kindness is what changes the world.

Growth is cyclical and ongoing. Linearity is not possible. There will be setbacks, deaths, births, rejuvenation, times of groundbreaking victory and times of unexplainable lulls. We must trust and embrace every part of this road back home to ourselves. We are the same, but different. We can no longer operate in the "ordinary world" as we did before so we must align ourselves in the best way possible.

I have met many people who are experts in their fields, niches, specialties, who cannot be told anything new. They know it all. They focus their lives on teaching their message, and sometimes become so passionate that they believe and advise their way as the only way. But to grow and evolve and continue learning, we must maintain a beginner's mind. Whether I am teaching a course, giving a talk, presenting a workshop, or leading a committee, I am still a student. We all have such varying gifts to offer one another, and our ongoing interactions facilitate the opportunity to continue exchanging ideas, energy, and passion. No matter how much you know about a subject—or how much you think you know—there is always more to learn. You can always make a choice to view things from an alternative perspective. This is the difference between knowledge and wisdom. When we stop learning, we stop growing, and more importantly, we can stunt others growth processes as well. All that I offer in this book are suggestions. Use what works, forget what doesn't. Take what you need, leave the rest.

We are always being tested to ensure we are capable of the mission with which we were entrusted. Every life event—challenge, interaction, blessing, synchronicity—presents itself for a reason. Sometimes, I want to look at the sky and scream, "Enough already! How much more do I have to go through? How many more lessons are there? Can I get a syllabus, at least?" It feels like that arcade game Whac-A-Mole. As soon as I feel stable with some semblance of control over my life (which is an illusion in itself), another incident or challenge or test or person pops up that needs to be dealt with.

We can't see it when we are deep in the weeds, but looking back and connecting the dots, we can usually figure out why something happened during a particular phase of our life, what it taught us, and how it strengthened our character.

Palm Trees and Purpose

Living in St. Croix was a significant part of my healing journey. Packing up and moving, ending my career with the federal government, enduring two Category-5 hurricanes within two months of my arrival, and carving a path for myself without anyone telling me what to do, where to go, who to be. These were all valuable life lessons that taught me I have the strength to overcome anything life throws at me.

I enjoyed living so simply and minimally—teaching yoga, working at the botanical garden gift shop, meeting interesting people, starting a health column for the local newspaper, slowing down and realizing what really matters in life, what really matters to *me*. This gave me the opportunity to fine-tune my value system, to disassociate from societal conditioning and faulty programming, and quiet things down enough to hear my inner voice. I learned that it was okay to sit under a palm tree for hours reading Tolstoy, and on some days I did just that. But, in the end, it wasn't enough for me. Something was missing. I loved my yoga students, writing for the island newspaper, and helping people in meaningful ways, but I knew my service could extend farther. I knew I wasn't living to my full potential, which is a recurring theme, and why I had taken off my white collar and left the safety and security of my past life in the first place.

I started to wonder, *Had I really gone through all I did just to sit alone off the grid musing and reflecting on the meaning of life?* It is a romantic concept, and I know in my bones that I needed that time and space to heal, but it got to a point where I realized I needed to be doing more and creating a greater impact in some way. I needed to use my story to help others. I was scared and didn't know how to go about that. So, I decided to go back to school and pursue a degree in Social Work.

It was time for the teacher to become the student again and learn how to use my skills, experience, and life lessons in a therapeutic setting.

Curve Ball

Bright eyed and bushy tailed, I was back in my element. Academia has always been a safe space for me, one in which I feel validated and gifted. I am in love with learning and, to be honest, I am quite good at it. By the second year of my master's program in Social Work, I finally felt like everything was falling into place. I was interning at a behavioral health unit of a renowned hospital and truly helping people. People like me. It blew my mind that I had made it to a point in my life where I had a badge to scan in and out of a psychiatric unit of the hospital. The patient was becoming the healer. My life had come full circle. Finally, I could use everything I went through to make a true difference in this world. Life made sense.

Then came the 13th day of October. It was just a normal Wednesday.

I was raped by a patient.[4]

Everything changed. I have had several transformative experiences in my life—battling anorexia, navigating bipolar disorder, stepping onto the path of recovery for alcoholism and addiction, literal hurricanes, and emotionally abusive relationships—but this one moment on that otherwise unremarkable Wednesday stands out as a distinct demarcation point. In a split second, my life became broken, and the chasm between the "before" and "after" reached far and wide. I couldn't close the gap. Things could never go back to the way they were.

I didn't set foot in that hospital again. I stopped going to my classes. Everything came to a halt. I was also going through a

---

[4] That is all I can say about this incident at present; merely typing those words took several weeks. Glennon Doyle, author of *Untamed*, says to write from our scars, not our open wounds, and this one is still bleeding.

tumultuous breakup at the time, so it felt like all the pillars of my existence, mired in my identity, were falling. I was stripped down and had to learn what was underneath it all to figure out where to go next.

I sank into a dark and scary hole. A few weeks after the incident, I remember stumbling across my dad's gun safe and realizing it was unlocked. I didn't pick it up, but I stared at it for a good while and thought to myself, *It is good to know that's accessible in case I ever need it.* I had a complete breakdown and confessed this episode to a victim support specialist to whom I had been referred by the forensics team at the hospital on the day of my attack. I was close to being hospitalized once again. But I decided in that moment that I was going to try to get better, just as I had done when I got sober. Here I was again, asking for help and strength from my higher power to get through the days and return to myself.

I am not alone in experiencing trauma or a life-changing event. All of us, to some degree, can relate to the feelings of devastation, loss, defeat, and confusion. I had to build myself back up. This meant keeping life very simple, but still moving forward. My psychiatrist said, "You were going 60 miles per hour, and now maybe you're down to 10 miles per hour, but you have to keep going. Don't come to a full stop." For almost a year, my victories were measured in drinking enough water, sleeping, showering, eating healthy, spending time with family, talking to people. I started creating my own therapeutic outpatient program. I took up guitar lessons, spent hours on intricate paint-by-numbers, and went to yoga classes—that covered my music, art, and movement therapy. I attended five to six recovery meetings a week for social support, got massages regularly, went for walks, adopted backyard chickens. And then there were times I stayed in bed all day binge-watching shows, crying on and off, and feeling sorry for myself, but I never came to a complete halt.

"One often meets his destiny on the road he takes to avoid it."
-Jean de La Fontaine

With my academic plans suddenly smashed and having sunk to a point where I literally had nothing to lose, I started stepping in different directions. Since nothing felt possible, anything was possible. I started taking writing classes like a mad woman and indulged in numerous creative projects. I joined the board of directors for a nonprofit vegan society in DC. I started participating in full moon circles at my yoga studio. I sought out social groups, communities, and organizations for things that excited me and figured out where I could lend a helping hand and become more involved. I even applied for and received a scholarship to participate in a writing and publishing workshop in Edinburgh, Scotland, and I went. My first time at such an event, and first time ever in Europe. Because, *why not?*

I remained open-minded and heart centered. Signs and synchronicity continued placing themselves in my periphery and directing each next moment. Even though I was scared and unsure, something was supporting me to stay devoted to my mission. Having no clue what the future held, or even what the next day would look like, I was winging it, which presented me the opportunity to fly.

Main Character Energy

We are the ones who stand in the way of our dreams. We resist what is naturally flowing to us, for many reasons. We think we are unworthy, that we don't deserve to live a certain way, we are incapable, people will judge us, we aren't good enough, we don't have enough time, it's too late. We can blame everyone and everything else, but that is the quickest way to give up your power and resign yourself to the role of the victim.

Our words and thoughts matter, and when self-esteem is low, we become malleable to the cues and triggers around us. We want to cause the least amount of disruption, so we act cool and try to seem laidback. I had spent my life trying to fit in with the crowd, playing small, coloring inside the lines, not ruffling any feathers, acting less intelligent and less interesting than I am. Operating that way, paralyzed by fear of judgment and ridicule, you become a servant to everyone around you, even strangers. Their thoughts and ideas become more important than your own, and thus you serve the role of a supporting character in everyone else's stories. To what end?

On the other hand, the main character is the one who takes chances. The one who excites us. Main characters don't have perfect lives, that's what drives a captivating plot along each twist and turn. Obstacles are thrown their way all the time. Overcoming and persevering in the face of those obstacles is what makes a story inspiring. If we are living in fear, we will choose any excuse over taking a risk. You can have excuses, or you can have results, but you can't have both.

You know how it feels when you're watching a movie and you're cheering on the main character in your head, believing in them in your heart, rooting for them? Start rooting for yourself. In this moment you have a choice—to let those fears knock you down and keep you down, whining with self-justification and self-pity, or to be the warrior who yet again courageously continues to face and survive the firing lines.

Make it fun. Make it a game. Play (Soul) Risk.

I had to start acting like the main character before I believed myself worthy. I started living intentionally, setting boundaries, and standing up for my decisions. I took up space. I took care of my body, mind, and soul. One I started treating myself and my life with unwavering worthiness, it became so embarrassingly obvious that we all have a right to decide our behaviors and actions in any given moment.

It sounds fairly straightforward, but there are all these nuances and unwritten rules embedded into society's norms and expectations—set by our family, partners, friends, schools, work, communities, and all other breeds of collective pressures.

Spirit Steps

Turn your Worry to Wonder.

Consider an area of your life that feels uncertain.
How can you turn that worry into wonder?
How can you look at it in a more playful and exciting way rather than planning your pain and dread?
Take several rounds of deep breaths, inhale through your nose and exhale through your mouth.
Set a timer for five minutes. What comes up?
Write down your insights.

Your job is to simply start trying new things and jumping in and trusting; the Universe will figure out the rest.

Simple Abundance

Magic hides in the mundane. As you Evolve, you will begin to find joy in everyday moments. When you are completely aligned and alive, committed to your growth and expansion, you will experience serenity. But you need to pay attention. There is no triumphant moment on a mountaintop to serve as the pinnacle of your life, where you will stand looking up at the heavens and think, *I have finally made it. My work here is done.* True transformation reveals itself in everyday abundance and simplicity—those little flashes in which we notice the radical change within ourselves. The feeling that we are living our truth is a freedom like no other, and we become inspired to embrace truth in all of life. You have always held this power within you, it just needs to be accessed.

The final step in the hero's journey is returning to the ordinary world with a hidden ingredient, a magical elixir, a treasure. This isn't only about you, and it never was. You have experienced a taste of freedom, and you now see that with this gift comes great responsibility. You shift your perspective from one of individual gain toward a universal mission. As you live in abundance and gratitude, the blessings will come faster than you can keep up with them. You will brim with compassion for others, as your cup has runneth over.

So, what will you do with that overflow?

Chapter Eight
Ascend

/ə-ˈsend/ verb
to move upward; to rise from a lower level or degree
They watched their balloons slowly *ascend* into the sky.

It's time to level up.

When the anxiety of purposelessness initially washed over me, the discomfort was more ego-based than anything else. I wanted to relieve my pain and anguish. I wanted to feel better about *my*self. It had nothing to do with anyone else. I just wanted to feel like my life meant more than how I spent my days. Luckily, that feeling is enough to know that you are being called by something greater.

I begged and begged the Universe to please reveal my purpose to me, as if one day a lightning bolt would strike me out of nowhere, making the path ahead clear and tidy, a manual that was easy to follow. I didn't understand that this difficult and painful journey of trying to find my purpose would ultimately become my purpose. Every twist and turn matters, nothing is wasted. Everything we go through is necessary to bring us to who and what we are today. You are given opportunity after opportunity to meet yourself on a level you may never had visited or a realm you wouldn't otherwise explore.

When you are living your truth and your passion, you are aligned with the Universe. You are collaborating with Spirit, and you show others that it is okay for them to be the main character of their own lives too. By being unapologetically yourself, using your voice, taking up space, showing your worth, you allow them to do the same.

For me, the gamechanger came with the realization that it wasn't all about me and my comfort, or my ego. *Oh, you're scared, Lindsey? Okay, well just stay in your room and get cozy. Pull down the shades. Don't daydream or imagine or wish. Don't put your words out there, even though you know they could be helping people. Stay small. Because that is familiar to you.*

I have heard that humility isn't thinking less of yourself, it's thinking of yourself less. It became too painful to stay hidden, wallowing in self-agony and confusion. After I was sexually assaulted at the hospital, I could have disintegrated. I could have stayed in a state of self-pity, reached for alcohol, and guzzled my brains out. I certainly had a justifiable reason to do so. I felt tempted to return to familiar unhealthy behaviors, like old friends you know you shouldn't be messing with anymore because you know where it will lead. But I couldn't live that way; it would just be another form of self-sabotage, a distraction. I looked at myself in the mirror and said out loud, "Don't do that. We can't ruin everything. We've come too far. Get it together, Lindsey." Because my higher self, my Spirit, knew that a downward spiral would be yet again another insidious detour from my true purpose.

There are so many ways I could have slowly and painstakingly destroyed my life. But I consciously made the decision to elevate to a new plane. It felt like a do-or-die moment, and at the same time a rising from the dead. I knew I was supposed to spread a message and answer the call I had ignored for so long. Instead of making decisions based on Lindsey's feelings and Lindsey's comfort and Lindsey's readiness, I started letting my mission make the call. Letting Spirit make the call. Does this person, place, thing, action support my greater purpose or detract from it? I set my ego aside. Discernment became easier, and eventually second nature. Life got simpler. Boundaries grew clearer. I realized everything I did or didn't do was one step closer or further away from aligning with Spirit and thus making the greatest impact possible, in a way that only I am capable of.

Spirit Steps

Here are some questions I asked myself, which I encourage you to consider:

What is a trivial task that could take me upward of three hours, but has nothing to do with what I am producing?

Stop doing it.

Who is the person becoming a crazy maker in my life, causing chaos and confusion, and robbing my peace?

Stop talking to them.

What places makes me feel weird and bring up bad memories?

Stop going there.

As you start to notice the moments you are out of alignment, consider your motive for engaging in that behavior, conversing with that person, or visiting that place. Stop what you are doing, take a few deep breaths, and then when you are in a safe space, write about it.

Acceptance and Authenticity

The more you are in a state of awareness and acceptance, the more you can use that information to Evolve. Over time, you will notice the misalignment more quickly, and you will begin to fluidly shift gears to course correct. Life isn't about never making mistakes, it is about responding and seeing them as lessons and continuing to move forward. Course-correcting. The rebound time will become faster, and you can make and act upon decisions more efficiently and with more trust in the Universe and more confidence in yourself.

Authenticity is more important than perfection. So much in my life changed for the better once I made a point to focus on helping and healing rather than impressing and winning. The ego is your brain talking, Spirit is your heart talking. If my need for approval outweighs my conviction to be my true self, then I will continue to fall short. I will send a flawed and surface-level message. I will revert back to prioritizing my comfort above all else, when in truth I am merely the vehicle and Spirit is the true author. If I don't let the Universe move through me in the way that is best to carry out my duties, then not only am I disrespecting my Creator, I'm also not getting the point across to the people who need to hear it most.

A student in a Reiki training I attended asked our instructor about the credibility of Reiki and how to defend the practice to skeptics who argue with its validity and reliability. "What if our clients say this…" or "What if they doubt that?" My Reiki master looked at us point blank and said, "The people who don't believe in this modality aren't who I am working for. I do this for the people who want to be healed."

These words stuck with me, and I aim to be strong enough to apply them to my own life. Yes, people will judge me, but those aren't the people I am trying to attract and help. They are none of my business and I am not worried about their thoughts. There are some authors out there that don't resonate with me and some that do. If you're pleasing everyone, you're doing something wrong. And if you're writing to everyone, you're writing to no one. So, by diluting my message to attempt to fit every single reader's standard (which is impossible anyway), I am not only failing to impress everyone, but I am also robbing the intended receivers of the message.

You Gotta Have Faith

Though we may not know where we will end up, for often we only see the next step and not the entire staircase, we can still maintain unwavering faith in the journey. We can remain devoted to our process without knowing the exact conditions of the outcome, without trying to control everything. Incorporating our personalized insights in the Allow phase of the journey, connecting with our version of Spirit, we can trust that everything is working out in our favor, that the Universe is conspiring for us. I spent years blocked off because I didn't understand intuition and soul. I thought all ideas and concepts had to come from the hard work of my own brainpower and I couldn't figure out how to do that perfectly, so I did nothing. I produced nothing. I couldn't put the words together to package anything meaningful. Analysis paralysis, some call it. But through letting go and creating space I can now realize and appreciate the art of it all and how Spirit plays a major role. Then, the inspiration starts to happen on its own.

Once I stopped worrying so much about the future and the output, the cause and effect, once I trusted the present moment in its own inherent right, the floodgates opened. When this happens, you must be ready. Ready to channel the water in the right direction, at the right speed, to the right place. You need to be fully present, which means you are enjoying the process rather than obsessing about the end game.

I often wake up in the middle of the night with ideas oozing out of my pores. I begrudgingly turn on the light, feel around for my glasses, and dig a pen and notebook out of my nightstand drawer to jot down my thoughts. Then I remind myself that this inspiration and guidance is what I so humbly begged for, and I thank the Universe for the artistry and insight to mold and structure my words in a way that can help others. Again, with power comes great responsibility.

If I am paying attention and staying present, I receive direct instructions on how to carry out my mission, how to fulfill my purpose. I keep a notebook with me everywhere I go. Even in places like yoga class. Especially in places like yoga class. Anytime we are in a liminal space or energetically charged atmosphere, ideas are bound to flow. It is our job to catch them in midair, like gentle wisps of wind. Let them flow around and through you. If you try to hoard these gifts and cling too tightly, if you aren't in a present state and are too worried about regretting the past and rehearsing for the future, the inspiration will be lost. You can't hold on to the wind.

Self-Awareness

You will start to become sensitive to contraindications, to interferences to your life path. By spending more time and energy in your lane of destiny, you will begin to feel the contrast of misalignment more clearly. You will sense when you are fighting a wave versus flowing with the stream. Allowing and surrendering and accepting will get you farther than controlling.

Resistance is a form of fear and control, constructed by the ego. The more we try to manipulate something, the less we are allowing Spirit in. If we are more worried about past mistakes for which we are embarrassed, and future happenings that could go wrong, we can't be present. In the present, there is no self-judgment or planning of pain that is to come, there is simply being here now and rising to the occasion. There is simply trusting and paying attention and delivering. There is simply love.

Law of Attraction (and Non-Attraction)

Most of the day-to-day work of transformation isn't sexy. It isn't always glamorous photos of peaceful meditation and green smoothies. There is grit involved. There is mess involved. There is a rearrangement of furniture, and we are bound to stub our toes and drop heavy objects. You are venturing deeper than most ever will. This path requires consistency, faith, and diligence.

Thoughts and words matter. Stop telling yourself, *It's going to be so hard.* Unless you want it to be hard, because then it will be. What if some parts of the journey could be fun and easy? Why not? If you are living your true purpose, shouldn't it be fun? Do the things that light up your soul. You can feel when you are in the zone and losing track of time. If you don't know what it is yet that makes you tick, start trying things, anything. The process of elimination is a very effective tactic. Collect data through trial and error for what works and what doesn't. Sometimes we must let go and unlearn before we can acquire new information and experience these intimate discoveries.

Your outer world reflects your inner world. It is not just ideas and things and concepts you will be attracting. The company you keep will begin to matter more. Critics exist within us and around us. Their insecurities are simply being projected onto you.

They are on their own journey, and it is not your job to convince them of your worth and coming success. You will start to naturally and effortlessly attract like-minded individuals whose paths you are meant to cross, whose messages you are meant to receive. Cultivate connections with those who believe in you, see you, hear you, support you.

Overflow

When you actively notice the beauty in your life, the rhyme and reason behind it all, the power and splendor of the Universe, you will have no other choice but to share that joy with others. You will seek out opportunities to extend gratitude by contributing to life's meaning.

I am in alignment with my purpose and committed to my path of helping as many people as possible. The Universe supports me in all ways. I am devoted to spreading my message. If something doesn't go "my" way, even if it is painful and not always easy, I trust that it is a redirection toward something better. Toward something I can't even dream up. That is when the miracles happen, not from me pushing and shoving and forcing things into place.

Before my healing journey started, I saw everything as so much work. I wanted to take creative risks but before I even got to any stages of action, I would gripe about everything that could go wrong, and how many steps were involved. I was too focused on my self-centered fear to see the big picture. Once I realized that I am building something that other people need and are relying on, the script flipped. My energy became boundless and my hope unstoppable.

Now I am constantly asking the Universe to show me how to be of service and give back, since I have been freely given so much. My life is wild in the best way. I welcome and experience all my feelings. I have a beautiful office to create and write and explore. I manage a wellness studio called Haven 101 that seemed to have appeared out of thin air, in a place where I least expected.

This space has given me a chance to offer my services. I facilitate guided meditations, lead creative workshops, teach yoga classes, work with my clients one-on-one, and collaborate with other amazing souls to spread truth. I don't feel a sense of competition, and the community is the most beautiful aspect of the whole operation. We come together by co-creating and integrating a variety of healing modalities ranging from spiritual creativity, massage therapy, nutrient IV infusions, energy healing, cacao ceremonies, full moon shamanic journeys, and many other interesting and unique services.

I am devoted to empowering others in their transformations because I understand the misery of feeling trapped and the joy of being free, and I believe everyone deserves the opportunity to choose which road they will take.

Epilogue
Infinity

/inˈfinədē/ noun
something that is unlimited, endless, without bound
Once at the summit, the view appears to stretch to *infinity*.

Congratulate yourself. I know how difficult change can be, and I wholeheartedly believe in you. You are not a problem to be fixed. You now have tools in your belt that will keep you going in the right direction. The right direction for *you*. One that leads you to pure truth and love. So that you can leave your unique imprint on this world. Remember to keep your batteries charged and the spark alive, even if some days burn a little dimmer than others. Self-care and nurturing are paramount and will reflect the quality of care you are capable of offering. Realize your power and energy, and never underestimate your ripple effect. Go forth and spread the light.

Though you have reached the end of this book, your journey has no end. That is what makes life so beautiful and mysterious. You will learn how to fine-tune your methods to more effectively and efficiently Notice, Allow, Shed, Unlock, Stabilize, Leap, Evolve, and Ascend. Whenever you feel lost, return to your breath, and then return to these words.

If your life starts feeling unmanageable and chaotic, go back to the basics of Notice and revisit Allow to enhance your connection to Spirit. When you feel overwhelmed by a pattern in your life that needs to be released, refer to Shed and identify what you can let go of. Are you experiencing a blockage to something deeper you could be accessing? Rediscover the powerful lessons of Unlock and let your energy flow. Does your routine need a boost in consistency and meaning? The tools of Stabilize will help you get back on track and make any adjustments necessary. For those moments in life when you may be facing a decision and want to know which road to take, Leap will help you tap into truth and discern fear and intuition. If you feel stunted in your growth and want to reach new levels of abundance and growth, review the concepts in Evolve. Finally, for the big picture where it all comes together, Ascend will raise you up to that sacred place of healing others through your journey. Remember who you are.

The precepts I offered at the beginning of this book can apply to your everyday life. They will help you stay on track:

Embrace curiosity instead of cynicism.

Look at it as an experiment, you are the sample.

Turn your worry into wonder.

Claim hope instead of doubt.

Be present, life is about paying attention.

Be gentle with yourself. Listen to yourself.

No one else knows you better than you do.

Let yourself have feelings and worries and emotions and never apologize for them.

Keep an open mind, a humble heart, and a receiving Soul.

Blessing

Please be you.
We need you.
You are the only person who can carry out your task for the world.
Now show us what you got, you beautiful soul you.
Peace and Love,
Linz

Acknowledgements

This book will forever hold a special place in my heart, as will the many people who have contributed to its evolution. To Tom, my best friend, biggest fan, protector, confidant, and first-round chapter reviewer—words cannot express what you mean to me. To my sister Jackie who is my angel. To my family for supporting my wild-child lifestyle (literally and figuratively). To my friends for making me laugh, cry, and everything in between. To those in the medical profession who have helped me come to a better place with my mental health and addictions. To all my fellows in recovery who will forever be by my side. To my healers and mentors, including my editor Wenonah Hoye, thank you for truly seeing me.

Explore
Research and Resources

/ik-ˈsplȯr/ verb
to investigate, study, or analyze: look into
I am ready to *explore* new ideas.

At my heart and soul, I am an academic. As such, I would be remiss to not share the research and theoretical principles from which the methods that form the framework of this book were derived. I created this section to give you the opportunity to dive deeper into the psychological and sociological concepts that drive behavior change. I've included parts of my story once again to serve as a backdrop for the science so that you can put a face to a name, so to speak, and see what this looks like in real life. While reviewing this section, consider how these ideas for exploration link with your own life and how you can use their interpretations to guide your personal journey.

Chapter One: Notice

Health Behavior Theory

The Stages of Change framework, also referred to as the Transtheoretical Model (TTM), has stood the test of time and been validated by countless peer-reviewed articles from scientists all over the world. Developed by James Prochaska and Carlo DiClemente in the late 1970s, the study first examined the experiences of smokers who quit on their own without requiring further treatment to understand why some people were capable and others weren't.[1] This model describes the process of intentional behavior change through a series of stages. It is widely used in various fields such as psychology, health promotion, and addiction treatment.

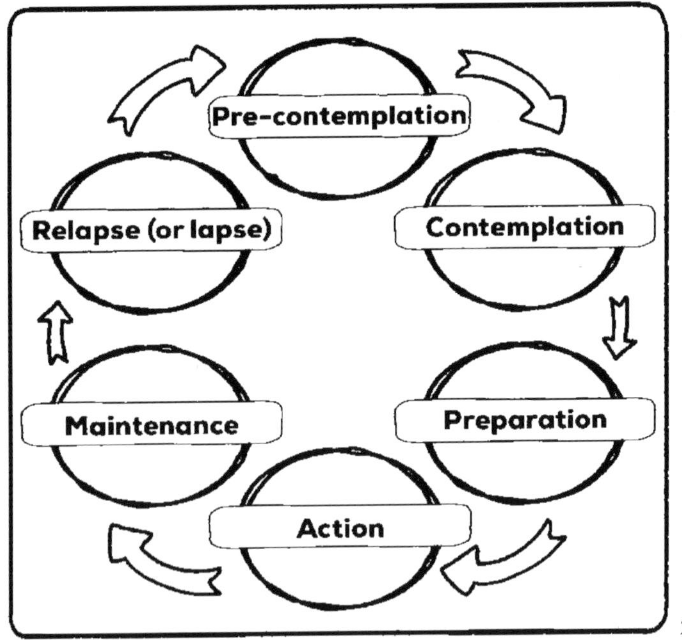

[2]

- *Precontemplation*: In this stage, individuals do not intend to take action in the foreseeable future, usually measured as the next six months. They may be unaware of the need to change or under-informed about the consequences of their behavior, though not necessarily. Often, we are well aware of our self-destructive behaviors, yet we choose (consciously or not) to stay in denial because the behavior is still serving some purpose—typically mental or emotional. Knowledge is rarely enough.

  Example: A smoker who is not considering quitting.[3]

  The first medical studies that warned of the dangers of smoking were published in Great Britain in the late 1940s, and here we are over eighty years later with 1.3 billion smokers worldwide.[4] In my own addiction, I spent years in the precontemplation phase. After my arrest for driving under the influence of alcohol, my probation protocol included watching videos weekly on the dangers of alcohol and drugs in a fluorescent-lit room near the courthouse. Learning more about their harm did nothing to move the needle on my addiction. I stayed in denial.
- *Contemplation*: Individuals in this stage recognize that they have a problem and start to think seriously about solving it. They intend to take action within the next six months. However, they are often ambivalent about change and still consider the pros and cons.

  Example: A smoker who is aware of the health risks and is thinking about quitting but has not yet made a commitment.
- *Preparation*: This stage combines intention and behavioral criteria. Individuals are intending to take action in the

immediate future, usually measured as the next month. They may begin taking small steps toward behavior change.

Example: A smoker who has decided to quit and has set a quit date or started reducing the number of cigarettes.

- *Action*: In this stage, individuals have made specific overt modifications in their lifestyles within the past six months. This is the stage where visible efforts are being made to change the behavior.

  Example: A smoker who has stopped smoking entirely within the last six months.

- *Maintenance*: Individuals in this stage have sustained their behavior change for a while, typically defined as six months or longer, and are working to prevent relapse. The focus is on maintaining the new behavior.

  Example: A former smoker who has not smoked for over six months and is focused on preventing relapse.

- *Relapse*: This stage refers to a time in a person's treatment where they have slipped back into old habits and returned to use. Relapse is said to happen when people lose sight of their goals. As a result of an inability to cope with current stressors, the person returns to an unhealthy addiction, instead of reaching out for help.

  Example: A former smoker who has not smoked for one year starts smoking again, amidst a difficult life-changing event.

This textbook model may look neat and tidy, but in practice it can take years for an individual to move from one stage to another. The growth process often requires looping back to previous lessons. Nevertheless, the Stages of Change Model provides a useful framework for understanding the process of behavior change and for designing interventions that are appropriate for individuals at different stages of the process.[5]

Depending on the individual stage of change, matching processes are proposed for supporting the individual's transition to the next stage.[6] For instance, moving from precontemplation to contemplation involves *consciousness raising* (i.e., seeking out and learning about ideas and ways of encouraging behavior change, aiming to make individuals aware of the need to alter their current behavior) and *risk assessment* (i.e., increased knowledge of comparing negative behavior with future positive behavior). These processes are akin to the Spirit Steps in the Notice phase of *Spirit Vigilante*; we collect the data and raise awareness around those behaviors. Positively framed interventions encourage a focus on successful behavioral change rather than on failure.

The transition from the contemplation stage to the preparation stage is an experiential process. *Self-reevaluation*[7] emphasizes that behavioral change is an important part of an individual's identity, which is basically an assessment of one's own self-image, or who one wants to be. In *Spirit Vigilante*, this process is mostly activated in the Unlock phase by taking an experiential approach to coming back to and remembering who we are. *Social support and self-efficacy* (situation-specific confidence)[8] help individuals cope with change. *Modeling* highlights following role-models who have previously overcome difficult barriers,[9] for example, answering the question "*How would _______ handle this situation?*" about someone you respect, follow, admire, or revere.

The transitions from preparation to action and from action to maintenance require behavioral processes to facilitate change. *Self-liberation,*[10] *f*or example, involves making a firm commitment to change, which is what this book is all about—deciding, planning, and staying the course. *Skill improvement*[11] refers to changing the existing environment in order to reinforce important, obvious, and socially supported clues, which are the main themes in Shed. In order not to "relapse" and revert to old, familiar, unhelpful thoughts and actions, it is important to be able to *cope with barriers.*[12] During this process, barriers are identified, and solutions as to how these can be circumvented are developed. This is why Stabilize is so important, so that we have a plan for how to handle day-to-day challenges, constantly fine-tuning and adjusting our coping skills to meet us where we are.

The Health Belief Model

The Health Belief Model (HBM) was originally formulated in the 1950s by social psychologists, Godfrey Hockbaum, Irwin Rosenstock, and others working in the U.S. Public Health Service to explain the failure of people participating in programs to prevent and detect disease.[13] Since then, it has been expanded upon and adapted to fit diverse cultural and topical contexts.

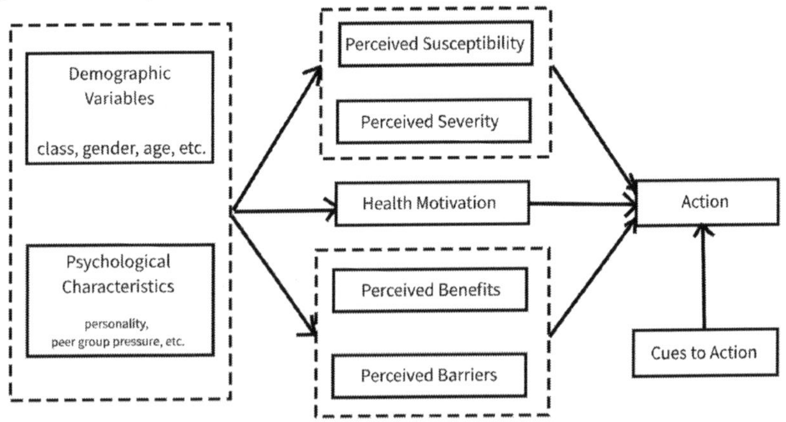

The constructs of the model for this stage of awareness are broken down into categories representing influences on one's likelihood to change their behavior through their perspective of the urgency and importance of modifying that particular lifestyle component. Needless to say, there are some overlaps in the HBM and the TTM frameworks. The Health Belief Model is still used today for disease prevention and health promotion, a classic example being observation of addiction and alcoholism and testing the effectiveness of protective behavioral strategies.[14]

1. *Perceived susceptibility* refers to a person's subjective perception of the risk of acquiring an illness or disease. There is wide variation in how people feel about their vulnerability to a disease, along with the consequences of continuing a specific behavior. For a long time, I did not think it possible that I could ever be or become an alcoholic because I had a very narrow perception of what that looked like. How could a successful woman in her twenties be an alcoholic? The prospect sounded ridiculous.
2. *Perceived severity* refers to a person's feelings on the seriousness of contracting an illness or disease (or the outcomes of leaving the illness or disease untreated). Often a person considers the medical consequences and social consequences (e.g., family life, social relationships) when evaluating the severity. I did not see my drinking and drug use as high-risk activities, and so felt no need to make any alterations in my lifestyle.
3. *Perceived benefits* refers to a person's perception of the effectiveness of various actions available to

reduce the threat of illness or disease (or to cure illness or disease). The course of action a person takes in preventing (or curing) illness or disease relies on consideration and evaluation of both perceived susceptibility and perceived benefit, such that the person would accept the recommended health action if it was perceived as beneficial. In other words, it wasn't until I realized the seriousness and danger of my alcoholism that I started looking at the positive reasons to lower my intake. That was all I could conceptualize at the time, as complete abstinence didn't seem possible.

4. *Perceived barriers* refers to a person's feelings on the obstacles to performing a recommended health action. The person weighs the effectiveness of the actions against the perceptions that it may be expensive, dangerous, unpleasant, time-consuming, or inconvenient. The barriers for treating addiction can range from socioeconomic limitations to worrying about how it might affect one's personal life and relationships. My own denial was fueled by a great fear of losing my friends and hobbies, as my life revolved around drinking.

5. *Cue to action* is the stimulus needed to trigger the decision-making process to accept a recommended health action. These cues can be internal (e.g., guilt, depression, the physical symptoms that accompany alcoholism, etc.) or external (e.g., advice from others, learning about the statistics of addiction, etc.). An example of an external cue to action was the advice from my therapist when he

suggested I experiment with abstinence and see if my life improved.

6. *Self-efficacy* refers an individual's confidence in his or her ability to successfully perform a behavior. Added to the model in the mid-1980s,[15] self-efficacy is now a construct in many behavioral theories because it directly relates to whether a person performs the desired behavior. I truly did not know if I could get better or not. It wasn't until I took that Leap of taking opposite action and found that I could be successful without drugs or alcohol that I felt empowered to fully commit to making this change.

Applying this model to my real-life scenario, one can clearly see that in the thick of my addiction, I did not believe that I was susceptible to becoming a full-blown alcoholic or that it was serious enough to contemplate change. Put more simply, I felt there was no point in fixing something that wasn't broken. Eventually, when I entered the space of Notice and began observing my behavior with an objective lens, I had to face the perceived benefits of changing my behavior (drinking alcohol) as well as the perceived barriers to fulfilling that commitment. I knew there would be uncomfortable, painful emotions running awry, as well as a complete conversion of thought processes and moral psyche, and an upending of my lifestyle overall.

Within the *Spirit Vigilante* methodology, cues to action primarily refer to the specific, positive stimuli that initiate or prompt a health behavior change[16] or strategies to activate "readiness." Cues to action are also relevant to the Leap phase when we start making changes based on intrinsic values, adapting our environments to accommodate those improvements.

Finally, self-efficacy, an important pillar in both the TTM as well as the HBM, is important throughout one's entire journey. Inextricably linked to this confidence is the ultimate touchstone: Faith. Especially in the Allow stage, we see the impact of holding an unwavering belief in something greater than ourselves. Staying devoted to a greater purpose, knowing that we can access that power at any time, allows us the stability and foundation to stay committed to truth.

Chapter Two: Allow

Health Outcomes and Spirituality

Maybe you're a stick-to-the-facts type of person. Perhaps you're wondering, *What place does spirituality have in science or health?* I can certainly relate. This is where open-mindedness and willingness come into play. If you truly are of such sound logical and rational mind, you can certainly appreciate this concept, as you understand the importance of proving a hypothesis null is just as important as proving it true. Who are we to ridicule an idea or claim prior to looking at all of the data?

In the words of philosopher Herbert Spencer, "There is a principle which is a bar against all information, which is proof against all arguments, and which cannot fail to keep a man in everlasting ignorance—that principle is contempt prior to investigation."

I can understand the negative stigma associated with mixing medical health and spirituality. At one point in the evolution of neurology and psychotherapy, religion was considered a symptom of mental illness—Jean Charcot and Sigmund Freud linked religion with neurosis, suggesting that religious and spiritual experiences are examples of psychopathology.[17] Though only less than a century ago, from a psychiatric standpoint those times might as well have been the dark ages. While both Charcot and Freud made significant contributions to the field of psychoanalysis, influencing subsequent high players such as Carl Jung, not everything they deducted can be held as gospel. In fact, recent research suggests the opposite. The importance of spirituality in mental health is now widely accepted, some experts and specialists going as far to say that religious belief is essential for psychiatric practice to be effective.[18] This checks out when we think about the roles of community and culture as integral factors of one's spiritual practices—churches, temples, mosques, and other places of gathering provide great comfort and safety to its members. People use spirituality to deepen their relationships with themselves and others, find comfort in difficult times, cultivate hope, live with more intention, and find purpose in life.

As heavily alluded to in the principles of Unlock, this search for meaning remains an enduring theme of the human condition. We have a universal trait of yearning to find significance and value in everyday life, making sense of it, connecting to ourselves and something greater, and integrating our own experiences with something more overarching and timeless than ourselves.[19]

Chapter Three: Shed

Cognitive Dissonance

As defined by Merriam-Webster, *cognitive dissonance* is the psychological conflict resulting from incongruous beliefs and attitudes held simultaneously. In other words, when you do something that goes against your values, it causes a disruption in your inner psyche. For example, maybe someone who works in the health and medical field frequently binge-drinks and feels this cognitive dissonance when advising their patients on the dangers of alcoholism. You enter a mental space of discomfort, angst, guilt, or shame associated with the decisions you're making and/or the beliefs you're questioning.

When this happens, either your behavior has to change or your values have to shift. For a long time, instead of admitting that my actions had fallen far outside of my moral bounds, my morals then had to change to accommodate the lifestyle I led. Cognitive dissonance isn't necessarily a negative thing. As with all emotional activity, we can see feelings as guideposts or indicators to make a change. You are at a crossroad and what you decide will determine who you want to be.[20]

Chapter Four: Unlock

Changing Beliefs

In the 1960s, Aaron Beck developed Cognitive Behavioral Therapy (CBT). Since then, it has been extensively researched and found to be effective in numerous outcomes studies for psychiatric disorders including depression, anxiety, eating disorders, bipolar disorder, and schizophrenia, substance abuse, and personality disorders, sometimes alone and sometimes as an adjunctive treatment to medication for the more serious conditions.[21]

Essentially, we are identifying the thought, as noted in Unlock, and then looking for the evidence or proof to support that thought. We usually discover that the original thought was distorted and are then able to develop a more accurate explanation. This helps override automatic thinking that negatively affects our feelings and behaviors. If we can catch the thought in the act, and do some cognitive restructuring, we can then pause and choose our response rather than react without thinking.

Common cognitive distortions have been developed to help identify irrational beliefs. Errors in logic are a common factor in patients with psychological disorders and these erroneous conclusions can become core beliefs.

Cognitive Distortions:

- *Dichotomous thinking*: Things are seen regarding two mutually exclusive categories with no shades of gray in between.

- *Overgeneralization*: Taking isolated cases and using them to make wide generalizations.

- *Selective abstraction*: Focusing exclusively on certain, usually negative or upsetting, aspects of something while ignoring the rest.

- *Disqualifying the positive*: Positive experiences that conflict with the individual's negative views are discounted.

- *Mind reading*: Assuming the thoughts and intentions of others.

- *Fortune telling*: Predicting how things will turn out before they happen.
- *Minimization*: Positive characteristics or experiences are treated as real but insignificant.
- *Catastrophizing*: Focusing on the worst possible outcome, however unlikely, or thinking that a situation is unbearable or impossible when it is just uncomfortable.
- *Emotional reasoning*: Making decisions and arguments based on how you feel rather than objective reality.
- *"Should" statements*: Concentrating on what you think "should" or "ought to be" rather than the actual situation you are faced with or having rigid rules which you always apply no matter the circumstances.
- *Personalization, blame, or attribution*: Assuming you are completely or directly responsible for a negative outcome. When applied to others consistently, the blame is the distortion. [22]

Using my own personal journey as a sample, I often become paranoid in assuming the thoughts and intentions of others (a consequence of the *mind reading* construct). This interferes with my self-esteem which then sets off a whole new set of challenges. If I were more realistic and took people at their word, I could let go of obsession and rumination and focus my energy elsewhere. I find that staying in the place of Ascend allows me to get out of my own head and focus on helping others which allows me to maintain a healthy sense of self-worth.

Underlying Beliefs:

Underlying beliefs shape our perception and interpretation of events. Belief systems or schemas take shape as we go through life experiences. They are defined as templates or rules for information processing that underlie the most superficial layer of automatic thoughts.[23]

Core Beliefs:

- The central ideas about self and the world.
- The most fundamental level of belief.
- They are global, rigid, and overgeneralized.

Examples of dysfunctional core beliefs:

- "I am unlovable."
- "I am inadequate."
- "The world is a hostile and dangerous place."

The nice thing about CBT is that it is solution-focused and goal-oriented, allowing the individual to take personal agency over their thoughts and feelings and often experience almost immediate results. The practices of Stabilize can help you stay on an even keel as you continue to Notice your tendencies to return to these negative places and Unlock a more truthful positive mindset to choose more constructive and positive behaviors.

Chapter Five: Stabilize

Health Outcomes and Social Support

In Western culture, we tend to wear independence and self-reliance as badges of honor. Early on, we are fed the theories on competitive advantage and our will to survive at all costs. We are shown time and time again that it is a dog-eat-dog world and we are trained to watch our backs. When we think about the infamous Charles Darwin's legacy of contributions to evolutionary biology, what usually first comes to mind is the concept of the "survival of the fittest." However, *The Descent of Man* only mentions this term twice and one of those instances is in admission that his earlier work on human evolution, the *Origin of Species*, perhaps attributed too much to survival of the fittest and natural selection.

Darwin explains that pure survival is the lowest of evolutionary drivers, outweighed by a number of other motivators as we advance along the evolutionary chain—ranging from sexual instincts on the lowest end to the Golden Rule on the highest, with parental instincts, social instincts, emotion and reason, and cultural habits falling somewhere in between.[24] (As a reminder, the Golden Rule is the principle of treating others as one would want to be treated.) Interestingly, as Darwin devalues certain elements of his original hypotheses on evolution, he uses the word "love" and the phrase "moral sensitivity" over 90 times each. Darwin goes on to say that man has retained instinctive love and sympathy for his fellows, and that confessing the happiness of others communicates a certain joy.

In the *Origin of Species*, Darwin writes, "As man is a social animal, it is almost certain that he would inherit a tendency to be faithful to his comrades, and obedient to the leader of this tribe; for these qualities are common to most social animals. He would consequently possess some capacity for self-command. He would from an inherited tendency be willing to defend, in concert with others, his fellow-men; and would be ready to aid them in any way, which did not too greatly interfere with his own welfare or his own strong desires" (1859).

Scientists have since found that as a species, along with many others in the animal kingdom, humans are naturally more democratic and conciliatory than we have been led to believe. Spirit resides in each and every one of us and thus we are all connected. By holding onto a rigid concept of individuality and uniqueness, we further separate ourselves from each other and from Spirit. We are more alike than we are different. We are here to help each other. When self-interest began to replace communal tendencies and cultural interdependence, our world began to suffer. The principles of Stabilize are so important because we need this social network and have the innate desire to help others. If we build and maintain these relationships, it will naturally lead to the outcomes of Ascend and freely sharing our gifts with the world. If you think this is just a lovey-dovey concept that sounds nice on paper, let's look at the science.

In the late 1950s and early 1960s, scientists discovered that people living in Roseto, Pennsylvania, were half as likely to die from a heart attack as folks from the neighboring town of Bangor, a mere 1.2 miles away. These two towns shared the same water supply, the same doctors and hospitals. There was no difference between their citizens in smoking status, occupation, or socioeconomic class. The most interesting detail about this is that Roseto residents weren't necessarily the paragon of wellness. In fact, scientists described them as obese and observed that they drank more alcohol and ate considerably more than the average American. So, what was the varying condition that separated these two geographical areas? The health status and low mortality rates of the residents of Roseto were attributed to the strength of their social connection as a community, the biggest predictor of longevity.[25]

With a population of only 1600 (approximately), among other study limitations, there may not be enough evidence to draw specific conclusions, though its implications certainly motivated future directions of study such as sociological determinants of health. Zooming out to a more modern and global perspective of the correlations between risk factors and lifestyle qualities, the infamous Blue Zones Project[26] has helped to uncover secrets of longevity by discovering the five geographical locations around the world where people consistently live to be over one hundred years old: Ikari, Greece; Okinawa, Japan; Sardinia, Italy; Loma Linda, California; and Nicoya, Costa Rica.

Led by author and longevity researcher Dan Buettner and his team of demographers, scientists, and anthropologists, the project distilled the evidence-based common denominators of these areas into commonalities, three of which involve community and social support: belonging to a community, usually faith-based (denomination does not seem to matter); social circles that support healthy behaviors; and putting family first, often involving multigenerational households and greater interdependence as a community.

Morning Rituals

Writing (Cleanse)

On top of improving one's mental health, journaling has also been proven to help regulate intense emotion, increase confidence, boost emotional intelligence, enhance critical thinking skills,[27] boost memory, improve physical health[28], and strengthen communication skills. Enhancing the ability of each person to take increasing personal responsibility for their own growth and development is a goal that has tremendous potential by encouraging a "proactive approach to the learning process."[29]

Writing and journaling have transformed my life. It allows a safe outlet to sort through my emotions and figure out productive ways to solve my problems. Let this be an ally in your healing as you consciously move through all the phases in this practice. I hope that you too will discover the power of writing.

Movement (Awaken)

It is common knowledge that improving one's physical health has a direct positive impact on mental and emotional health by releasing endorphins that relieve stress, allowing us to take a break from everyday challenges, increase mindfulness, providing an outlet for self-expression, helping emotions move through our bodies, and strengthening the mind-body connection.[30] I see movement as part of my medicine to keep me stable and healthy.

Breathwork (Breathe)

Breath is life so it is no wonder that there are so many benefits to conscious breathwork: stress reduction, improved focus and concentration, enhanced emotional regulation, better sleep, improved lung function, healthier digestion, and pain management.[31]

Spiritual Connection (Ask)

Prayer is to the mind-soul connection as movement is to the mind-body connection. It is a difficult topic to study because one cannot isolate the conditions to determine which part of the prayer process is benefitting us—the moment of stillness, the words conjured, the faith community? Nevertheless, the ritual of prayer has been shown to reduce feelings of isolation, anxiety and fear.[32]

The philosopher Blaise Pascal suggested that since it is not possible to prove or disprove that God exists, it is more advantageous to bet that God does in fact exist and therefore live accordingly as a form of potential harm reduction. That is a very structural way of viewing an abstract concept, and while I am not encouraging you to take that bet, I am encouraging you to practice living accordingly and see where the laws of Pascal's wager take you.

Meditation (Listen)

Research has confirmed a host of health benefits associated with the practice of meditation: decreased anxiety, decreased depression, pain reduction, improved memory, increased efficiency, and physiological benefits (reduced blood pressure, heart rate, and cortisol). Meditation is also associated with an increase in gray matter in the brain, which is the opposite of the aging process in which the brain's cortical thickness (gray matter which contains neurons), decreases. Efficacy of meditation techniques has been found for epilepsy, symptoms of premenstrual syndrome and menopause. Benefits have been demonstrated for mood and anxiety disorders, autoimmune illness, and emotional disturbances.[33]

There is no doubt that meditation is inherently difficult. Just remember there is no wrong way to do it and you are just experimenting to find out if meditation might be a variable to test and determine the potential benefit to your journey. If not, let it go. But at least give it a try. If you don't, you will never know.

Self-Efficacy

Albert Bandura's theory of self-efficacy has been applied in many areas of health education including smoking cessation, pain control, eating problems, cardiac rehabilitation, and adherence to regimens. Self-efficacy is the connection between knowledge and action since the belief that one can do a behavior usually occurs before one attempts the behavior.[34] Bandura explained that it is not enough for individuals to possess the requisite knowledge and skills to perform a task; they also must have the conviction that they can successfully perform the required behavior(s) under typical and, importantly, under challenging circumstances.[35]

Chapter Six: Leap

Synchronicity

Defined by Carl Jung as "unpredictable occurrences of meaningful coincidence,"[36] *synchronicity* refers to unusual events linking the internal and external worlds of the individual—meaning something more than mere chance. The acknowledgement of synchronicity is beneficial in therapeutic settings as well as in understanding career pathways and processes.[37]

An external experience is given meaning when it is connected to a person's inner world. While the term synchronicity is usually seen through the lens of spirituality, findings of a report that developed and validated a tool for synchronicity awareness and meaning-detection suggest that these constructs are positively associated with openness to experience and tolerance for ambiguity.[38] It all comes back to man's search for deeper meaning and purpose, concepts of Allow, Unlock, Stabilize, Leap, and Ascend.

Synchronicity awareness is possibly a mediator for the complex relation between the search for meaning and life satisfaction. Individuals who are open to synchronicity events tend to experience more optimism, which may be cultivated by regaining a sense of order and coherence. It was found that when contemplating future decisions in business and leadership, individuals have relied on the principle of synchronicity,[39] suggesting this open-minded view may enhance positive expectations of the future.

I had to put the logical part of my brain aside (not too far away as I still needed it to help me organize) to trust the signs that prompted my move to St. Croix. I believe that synchronicity is woven into the fabric of time and space to put us right where we need to be to receive specific messages.

Chapter Seven: Evolve

Abraham Maslow's Hierarchy of Needs

Often, I find myself asking, "Why does the state of my psyche matter when people are starving? How can I feel depressed when others are homeless? Why can't I just be grateful for everything I *do* have?" This feeling of unrest is not a negative signal. Social psychologists have proven that once our basic needs are met, our goals adjust and advance. Once we have food and safety, we then need to feel a sense of love and belonging, followed by self-esteem and fulfillment.[40] We are being called to live rewarding lives because there is something meant for us to fulfill in this world.

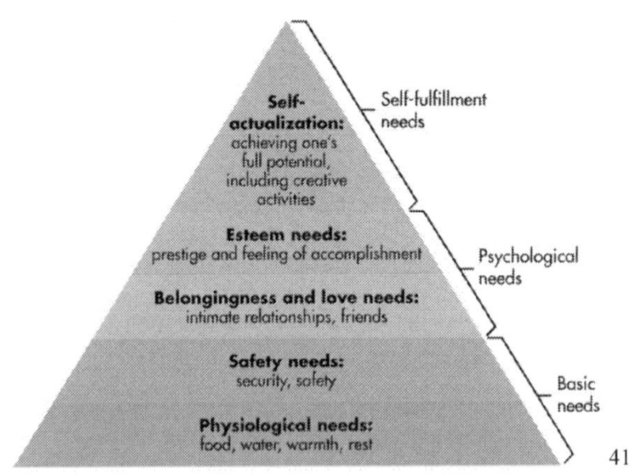

[41]

Many of us struggle with the concept of privilege, which is where this process of self-interrogation enters. We see self-discovery as a luxury unaffordable to others, so why should we enjoy that advantage and benefit? The fact is we need to put our oxygen mask on first because then we will be able to best serve those around us. The Universe wants us to carry out our missions and share our fortune, tools, and resources to help others. Gratitude for all that you have can exist in tandem with the transformation process, and the truth is that this journey on which you embark is the best gift in the world. The Ascend phase helps us to fully embody this universal truth.

Chapter Eight: Ascend

The Law of Attraction

When I first entered recovery, my self-esteem was at an all-time low. Someone told me, "If you want to raise your self-worth, do worthy things." In other words, mood follows action. We all know how good it feels to do a kind deed for another, the positive experience of generosity that nothing can quite match. We don't necessarily need a principal investigator to prove that to us, but if you are interested, there does exist a neural link between generosity and happiness.

"Generosity" is defined as the act of giving without expecting anything in return. In virtually all religions, generosity is rewarded, and in Buddhism, it is thought to be the opposite of greed.[42] As human beings we enjoy feeling useful, we enjoy contributing to the world around us. We want a reason to wake up in the morning. By increasing our self-worth, we are enhancing our abilities to attract and receive what we feel we truly deserve.

The phenomena of manifestation and the Law of Attraction have become popular topics of discussion. With documentary films such as *The Secret* and thought leaders like Joe Dispenza and Deepak Chopra, the messaging can seem overwhelming. Trying to figure out how to make it all work rather than simply allowing goodness into our lives. I find it helpful to start with smaller steps rather than grand declarations of power and allure, though I believe such results are also possible. Greg Braden, author of the *Divine Matrix* writes that in each moment of the day we make choices that either affirm or deny our lives. We are either nourishing ourselves in a way that supports our journey or depleting our energy.[43] Something as simple as speaking about other people in an honoring versus dishonoring manner can have powerful effects on our inner energy and thus the manifestation of our outer world.

Putting It All to Practice

With so much emphasis on self-discovery and becoming the main character of your life, putting others first may feel paradoxical. One minute we are learning about boundaries and the next we are told to lend a helping hand. Oddly enough, the two are inextricably linked. Our identity is formed through our interactions with our peers in the community—at both the microlevel and macrolevel. Mahatma Gandhi said, "The best way to find yourself is to lose yourself in the service of others." We want to feel we are contributing to those around us, that we serve a purpose in our society—whether that be with family, friends, or largescale organizations. These two concepts work in tandem—a delicate dance with the Universe, giving and receiving.

Fundamental knowledge of the psychological precepts and foundational frameworks of behavior change are critical to understanding the underlying patterns of the human psyche and how we operate, so that we may effectively promote and implement healthy lifestyle modifications. Remember that denial and ignorance keep us stuck, and self-discovery is the secret antidote. Allow your own findings and interpretations of the *Spirit Vigilante* lessons to serve as a steady base to build upon as you conduct your own in vivo experiment. Armed with the meanings, origins, and evidential outcomes behind these key suggestions for healing, you have strengthened your self-efficacy, more clearly defined your core values, and may now move through life with confidence and conviction of your place in this world.

Bibliography

[1] Prochaska, James O., Wayne F. Velicer, Carlo C. DiClemente, and Joseph Fava. "Measuring Processes of Change: Applications to the Cessation of Smoking." *Journal of Consulting and Clinical Psychology* 56, no. 4 (August 1, 1988): 520–28. https://doi.org/10.1037/0022-006x.56.4.520.

[2] Webb, Mitchell. "The Stages of Change Model." The Stages of Change Model – Webb Therapy. Accessed September 19, 2024. https://webbtherapy.org/the-stages-of-change-model.

[3] Prochaska, James O., Wayne F. Velicer, Carlo C. DiClemente, and Joseph Fava. "Measuring Processes of Change: Applications to the Cessation of Smoking." *Journal of Consulting and Clinical Psychology* 56, no. 4 (August 1, 1988): 520–28. https://doi.org/10.1037/0022-006x.56.4.520.

[4] World Health Organization. "Tobacco Fact Sheet." *Wntd-Tobacco-Fact-Sheet.Pdf.* World Health Organization (WHO). Accessed September 19, 2024. https://www.who.int/docs/default-source/campaigns-and-initiatives/world-no-tobacco-day-2020/wntd-tobacco-fact-sheet.pdf.

[5] Friman, Margareta, Jana Huck, and Lars Olsson. "Transtheoretical Model of Change During Travel Behavior Interventions: An Integrative Review." *International Journal of Environmental Research and*

Public Health 14, no. 6 (May 30, 2017): 581. https://doi.org/10.3390/ijerph14060581.

[6] Raihan, Nahrain, and Mark Cogburn. "Stages of Change Theory." StatPearls - NCBI Bookshelf, March 6, 2023. https://www.ncbi.nlm.nih.gov/books/NBK556005/.

[7] Raihan, Nahrain, and Mark Cogburn. "Stages of Change Theory." StatPearls - NCBI Bookshelf, March 6, 2023. https://www.ncbi.nlm.nih.gov/books/NBK556005/.

[8] Raihan, Nahrain, and Mark Cogburn. "Stages of Change Theory." StatPearls - NCBI Bookshelf, March 6, 2023. https://www.ncbi.nlm.nih.gov/books/NBK556005/.

[9] Raihan, Nahrain, and Mark Cogburn. "Stages of Change Theory." StatPearls - NCBI Bookshelf, March 6, 2023. https://www.ncbi.nlm.nih.gov/books/NBK556005/.

[10] Raihan, Nahrain, and Mark Cogburn. "Stages of Change Theory." StatPearls - NCBI Bookshelf, March 6, 2023. https://www.ncbi.nlm.nih.gov/books/NBK556005/.

[11] Raihan, Nahrain, and Mark Cogburn. "Stages of Change Theory." StatPearls - NCBI Bookshelf, March 6, 2023. https://www.ncbi.nlm.nih.gov/books/NBK556005/.

[12] Raihan, Nahrain, and Mark Cogburn. "Stages of Change Theory." StatPearls - NCBI Bookshelf, March 6, 2023. https://www.ncbi.nlm.nih.gov/books/NBK556005/.

[13] Rosenstock, Irwin M. "The Health Belief Model and Preventive Health Behavior on JSTOR." *Www.Jstor.Org* 2, no. 4 (season-04 1974). http://www.jstor.org/stable/45240623.

[14] De Leon, Ardhys N., Roselyn Peterson, Robert D. Dvorak, Angelina V. Leary, Matthew P. Kramer, Emily K. Burr, Ethan M. Toth, and Daniel Pinto. "The Health Belief Model in the Context of Alcohol Protective Behavioral Strategies." *Psychiatry* 86, no. 1 (October 14, 2022): 1–16. https://doi.org/10.1080/00332747.2022.2114270.

[15] Jones, Christina L, Jakob D Jensen, Courtney L Scherr, Natasha R Brown, Katheryn Christy, and Jeremy Weaver. "The Health Belief Model as an Explanatory Framework in Communication Research: Exploring Parallel, Serial, and Moderated Mediation." *Health Communication* 30, no. 6 (July 10, 2014): 566–76. https://doi.org/10.1080/10410236.2013.873363.

[16] Meillier, Lucette K., Anker Brink Lund, and Gerjo Kok. "Cues to Action in the Process of Changing Lifestyle." *Patient Education and Counseling* 30, no. 1 (January 1, 1997): 37–51. https://doi.org/10.1016/s0738-3991(96)00957-3.

[17] Verghese, Abraham. "Spirituality and Mental Health." *Indian Journal of Psychiatry* 50, no. 4 (January 1, 2008): 233. https://doi.org/10.4103/0019-5545.44742.

[18] Turbott, John. "Religion, Spirituality and Psychiatry: Conceptual, Cultural and Personal Challenges." *Australian & New Zealand Journal of Psychiatry* 30, no. 6 (December 1, 1996): 720–27. https://doi.org/10.3109/00048679609065037.

[19] McLean Hospital. "Understanding Spirituality and Mental Health | McLean Hospital," 2024. Accessed September 19, 2024. https://www.mcleanhospital.org/essential/spirituality.

[20] Clinic, Cleveland. "What Is Cognitive Dissonance?" Cleveland Clinic, June 27, 2024. https://health.clevelandclinic.org/cognitive-dissonance.

[21] Chand, S, DP Kuckel, and MR Huecker. *Cognitive Behavioral Therapy.* StatPearls Publishing. 2023.

[22] Chand, S, DP Kuckel, and MR Huecker. *Cognitive Behavioral Therapy.* StatPearls Publishing. 2023.

[23] Chand, S, DP Kuckel, and MR Huecker. Cognitive Behavioral Therapy. StatPearls Publishing. 2023.

[24] Darwin, Charles. *The Descent of Man, and Selection in Relation to Sex. John Murray,* 1871.

[25] Egolf, B, J Lasker, S Wolf, and L Potvin. "The Roseto Effect: A 50-year Comparison of Mortality Rates." *American Journal of Public Health* 82, no. 8 (August 1, 1992): 1089–92. https://doi.org/10.2105/ajph.82.8.1089.

[26] Buettner, Dan, and Sam Skemp. "Blue Zones." *American Journal of Lifestyle Medicine* 10, no. 5 (July 7, 2016): 318–21. https://doi.org/10.1177/1559827616637066.

[27] Raterink, Ginger. "Reflective Journaling for Critical Thinking Development in Advanced Practice Registered Nurse Students." *Journal of Nursing Education* 55, no. 2 (February 1, 2016): 101–4. https://doi.org/10.3928/01484834-20160114-08.

[28] Baikie, Karen A., and Kay Wilhelm. "Emotional and Physical Health Benefits of Expressive Writing." *Advances in Psychiatric Treatment* 11, no. 5 (August 31, 2005): 338–46. https://doi.org/10.1192/apt.11.5.338.

[29] Brockett, Ralph G., and Roger Hiemstra. *Self-Direction in Adult Learning*, 1991. https://doi.org/10.4324/9780429457319.

[30] University of Colorado Boulder. "Mental Health is... Moving Your Body." Mental Health Is... Moving Your Body | Health & Wellness Services | University of Colorado Boulder, May 20, 2024. Accessed September 19, 2024. https://www.colorado.edu/health/blog/moving-your-body.

[31] De Montjoye, Cat. "The Power of Breath: The Surprising Benefits of Conscious Breathing - DHW Blog." DHW Blog, September 15, 2023. https://dhwblog.dukehealth.org/the-power-of-breath-the-surprising-benefits-of-conscious-breathing/.

[32] Rogers, Kristen. "The Psychological Benefits of Prayer: What Science Says About the Mind-Soul Connection." The Psychological Benefits of Prayer | CNN, June 17, 2020. Accessed September 19, 2024. https://edition.cnn.com/2020/06/17/health/benefits-of-prayer-wellness/index.html.

[33] Sharma, Hari. "Meditation: Process and effects." *AYU (an International Quarterly Journal of Research in Ayurveda)* 36, no. 3 (January 1, 2015): 233. https://doi.org/10.4103/0974-8520.182756.

[34] Lawrance, L, and KR McLeroy. "Self-efficacy and Health Education." *The Journal of School Health* 56, no. 8 (1986): 317-21. doi:10.1111/j.1746-1561.1986.tb05761.x.

[35] Albert Bandura. *Self-efficacy: The Exercise of Control.* W. H. Freeman and Company, 1997.

[36] C. G. Jung. *Synchronicity: An Acausal Connecting Principle.* Vol. 8. Bollingen Series: Princeton University Press, 1969. https://s3.us-west-1.wasabisys.com/luminist/EB/I-J-K/Jung%20-%20Synchronicity.pdf.

[37] Connolly, Angela. "Bridging the Reductive and the Synthetic: Some Reflections on the Clinical Implications of Synchronicity." *Journal of Analytical Psychology* 60, no. 2 (March 23, 2015): 159–78. https://doi.org/10.1111/1468-5922.12142.

[38] Russo-Netzer, Pninit, and Tamar Icekson. "An Underexplored Pathway to Life Satisfaction: The Development and Validation of the Synchronicity Awareness and Meaning-Detecting Scale." *Frontiers in Psychology* 13 (January 16, 2023). https://doi.org/10.3389/fpsyg.2022.1053296.

[39] Laveman D. "Business Leadership, Synchronicity, and Psychophysical Reality," in *The Pauli-Jung Conjecture and Its Impact Today*, edited by Harald Atmanspacher and Christopher A. Fuchs. Imprint Academic, 2014.

[40] Hamilton, John. "Abraham Maslow Humanistic Psychology & Theory | Who was Abraham Maslow?," November 21, 2023. Accessed September 19, 2024. https://study.com/academy/lesson/abraham-maslows-contribution-to-the-humanistic-movement-in-psychology.html.

[41] McLeod, Saul. "Maslow's Hierarchy of Needs," January 24, 2024. Accessed October 20, 2024. https://www.simplypsychology.org/maslow.html

[42] Castillo, M. "A Call to Action: Maintain Your Happiness, Be Generous!" *American Journal of Neuroradiology* 35, no.

8 (November 7, 2013): 1447–48. https://doi.org/10.3174/ajnr.a3775.

[43] Braden, Gregg. *The Divine Matrix: Bridging Time, Space, Miracles, and Belief*. Hay House LLC, 2008.

Made in the USA
Columbia, SC
06 April 2025

cd2bdcd3-1e88-4c8e-829b-5e148de76018R01